Easy Weekends

Easy Weekends

FOOD BY NEIL PERRY

Photography by
Earl Carter

Styling and direction by
Sue Fairlie-Cuninghame

MURDOCH BOOKS

To my darlings, Macy and Indy.
A healthy and happy life can be lived
through good food.

Contents

Good shopping,
good cooking, good living
has always been my mantra.

My hope is that this book helps you cook, inspires you to buy quality ingredients and makes you want to cook for your friends and family. Nothing in life is more beautiful to me than sharing a meal with the people I love; it is what I live for.

I believe the way to a healthy life is through a well-balanced diet comprising fresh food and variety. Nothing is really bad for you in moderation. I love pork fat, but do I eat it every day? No, of course not. Do I enjoy it as a treat in my bacon for breakfast or in an Asian stir-fry or braise? Yes, most definitely. Moderation is the key to good eating; balance your diet with fruit, vegetables, grains, nuts, dairy and a good amount of fish. Then the big juicy steak, the chicken skin, the butter and a bit of pork fat won't hurt you. And boy oh boy is there flavour in those amazing ingredients.

Marry fresh food with a bit of daily exercise and you have the blueprint for a happy healthy life. You don't need to go to the gym every day, just go for a morning walk or run up the stairs at work; don't always take the elevator in life. Drink plenty of water, and wine in moderation. I should listen to my own advice…

You can prepare most of these recipes without being an amazingly-skilled cook. I want this book to be approachable, to give you simple ideas that work well together. I hope it helps you explore the different cuisines that have always influenced my food. It is Australia's multiculturalism that has defined me as a cook and I want to share some of those Eastern and Western influences, which have made me who I am.

A final word from me on becoming a better cook. If you enjoy it, simply cook more often and take notice of what you do. Try and remember if the fish was perfectly cooked last time and make a note if the chicken was a little overcooked. Was the oven too hot? Did I cook it for ten minutes too long? Every time you cook you can learn something — every day. If you can be bothered, keep a little notebook and jot down what happened and how to make it better next time. It makes for an amazing read after a couple of years. Imagine your grandchildren's delight when they discover grandma's or granddad's little kitchen notebook …

Happy cooking is about memory, love, happiness and life.

Neil

Friday

Italian-style zucchini and parmesan soup

Most vegetables can be used to make a delicious puréed soup like this. My favourites include cauliflower, Jerusalem artichoke, parsnip and pea.

SERVES 4

+ Heat a little olive oil in a heavy-based saucepan over medium heat, then add the zucchini, garlic, basil and a good pinch of sea salt. Cook, stirring occasionally, for about 10 minutes or until the zucchini starts to soften.

+ Add the stock and bring to the boil, then reduce the heat to low and simmer for about 8 minutes or until the zucchini is soft and the stock is slightly reduced.

+ Pour the soup into a blender and pulse until well puréed, but not completely smooth if you want the soup to have a bit of texture. Return the soup to the pan and stir in the cream, butter and parmesan. Season to taste.

+ Divide the soup among four bowls, add a good grind of white pepper and sprinkle with the extra parmesan. I like to add an extra splash of cream to each bowl to finish.

750 g (1 lb 10 oz) green zucchini (courgettes), trimmed and cut into 1 cm (½ inch) pieces
extra virgin olive oil
6 garlic cloves, finely chopped
85 g (3 oz/1 bunch) basil, leaves picked
sea salt and freshly ground white pepper, to taste
1.5 litres (52 fl oz/6 cups) chicken stock
125 ml (4 fl oz/½ cup) thin (pouring/ whipping) cream, plus extra, to serve (optional)
40 g (1½ oz) unsalted butter, chopped
40 g (1½ oz) parmesan, grated, plus extra, to serve

NOTES

If you use different vegetables cooking times will vary, so if the vegetables take longer to soften, add more stock or water.

Use freshly grated parmesan — not the pre-grated stuff!

Cream of fennel soup

You can make this soup heartier by adding a grilled or toasted crouton rubbed with garlic, and drizzled with extra virgin olive oil.

SERVES 4

+ Heat 50 g (1¾ oz) of the butter and the olive oil in a saucepan over medium heat until the butter starts to foam. Add the leek, shallots and a little sea salt and cook for 5–6 minutes until the vegetables start to soften. Add the stock and fennel and bring to the boil, then reduce the heat to low and simmer for 30 minutes.

+ Purée the soup in batches in a blender. If you want to, now is the time to pass the soup through a sieve for a finer texture. Heat the purée and cream in a pan, check for seasoning and add more sea salt if necessary.

+ Sauté the bacon in a frying pan over medium heat until crispy, add the sage leaves and the remaining butter then cook the butter until it is nut brown and the sage is crisp.

+ Divide the soup among four bowls, top with the bacon and sage and add a good grind of white pepper.

500 g (1 lb 2 oz) fennel, washed and trimmed, cut into 1 cm (½ inch) dice
120 g (4¼ oz) unsalted butter
2 tablespoons extra virgin olive oil
2 small leeks, white part only, washed and finely chopped
4 French shallots, finely chopped
sea salt and freshly ground white pepper, to taste
1 litre (35 fl oz/4 cups) chicken stock or water
125 ml (4 fl oz/½ cup) thin (pouring/ whipping) cream
2 rashers bacon, chopped
8 sage leaves

NOTES

Adding herbs is also a really nice thing to do to enhance the flavours of the soup.

A dash of Pernod would take this soup to another level.

Seared Hiramasa kingfish salad

While I have used kingfish in this recipe, any fish or shellfish you love raw will work a treat with this salad.

SERVES 4

Sesame dressing

3 tablespoons Japanese sesame paste
1 tablespoon caster (superfine) sugar
2 tablespoons soy sauce
2 tablespoons rice vinegar
2 tablespoons mirin
1 tablespoon red chilli paste
2 tablespoons coarsely ground
   sesame seeds

400 g (14 oz) block sashimi-quality
   Hiramasa kingfish fillet
sea salt and freshly ground white pepper
2 teaspoons vegetable oil
250 g (9 oz) mixed green salad leaves,
   washed and dried
1 ripe avocado, thinly sliced
2 red Asian shallots, thinly sliced
toasted sesame seeds, to serve (optional)

+ To make the dressing, place all the ingredients and 80 ml (2½ oz/⅓ cup) hot water in a bowl and whisk to combine well. Season to taste with white pepper and set aside.

+ Season the fish fillet with sea salt and white pepper to taste.

+ Heat the oil in a heavy-based frying pan over medium–high heat until just smoking and sear the fish on all sides until it has a nice golden brown colour but is still nice and raw throughout. Set the fish aside to rest.

+ Divide the salad leaves among four plates, then place the avocado on the leaves and add the shallots.

+ With a sharp knife, cut the fish into thin, even slices. Place the fish on the salad and spoon the dressing liberally over the fish and leaves. Sprinkle with extra toasted sesame seeds, if desired, season the fish with salt and a grind of white pepper and serve.

NOTES

It is well worth having the Japanese staples of soy sauce, rice wine, mirin and pickled ginger in the pantry.

If you can find shiso leaves, they are a fantastic spicy addition to this salad.

King prawn and white bean salad with lemon anchovy dressing

This salad is also fantastic with lobster, crab or scallops. Instead of the beans, try chickpeas, lentils or any other pulse.

SERVES 8

+ To make the dressing, mash the anchovies, garlic and a little white pepper in a mortar with a pestle. Slowly pound in the olive oil, lemon juice and then, finally, the herbs until you have a thick green slush. Check the seasoning.

+ In a bowl, gently toss the radicchio with one-third of the dressing then arrange the leaves in the centre of a large platter or eight plates.

+ Place the beans, prawns and remaining dressing in the bowl and toss gently. Pile onto the platter or divide among the plates and sprinkle with sea salt and a grind of white pepper.

NOTES

I also add blanched green beans, peas or asparagus, or braised artichokes when they're in season.

This salad would go nicely with a wonderful aromatic wine — a very dry riesling would be my pick.

32 cooked king prawns (shrimp), peeled and deveined
2 radicchio hearts, leaves separated and torn
2 x 400 g (14 oz) tins white beans, drained and rinsed

Lemon anchovy dressing

6 anchovy fillets, finely chopped
4 garlic cloves, finely chopped
sea salt and freshly ground white pepper
200 ml (7 fl oz) extra virgin olive oil
2 tablespoons lemon juice
2 handfuls basil leaves, torn
2 handfuls mint leaves, finely chopped
1 large handful flat-leaf (Italian) parsley leaves, roughly chopped

Spicy roast chicken, mango and macadamia salad

This is a simple, delicious summer salad, making the most of sweet Australian ingredients at their seasonal peak, together with chicken — one of my favourite proteins.

SERVES 4

1 free-range roast chicken (organic if possible), bones removed, meat sliced (see Note)
2 firm but ripe mangoes, peeled and cut into bite-sized chunks
2 Lebanese (short) cucumbers, halved lengthways and sliced on the diagonal
10 cherry tomatoes, quartered or halved
4 French shallots, halved and thinly sliced
1 radicchio heart, sliced (or red witlof if you can get it)
1 handful coriander (cilantro) leaves
1 small handful mint leaves
2 spring onions (scallions), sliced on the diagonal

110 g (3¾ oz/⅔ cup) macadamia nuts, roasted until lightly golden and sliced or roughly chopped

Chilli lime dressing

1 garlic clove, crushed
1 teaspoon mild chilli flakes
1 tablespoon caster (superfine) sugar
juice of 2 limes
100 ml (3½ fl oz) extra virgin olive oil
sea salt and freshly ground black pepper

+ To make the dressing, combine all the ingredients in a bowl and season with salt and pepper. It should be sharp and hot, with a nutty balance from the olive oil.

+ For the salad, put all the ingredients, except the nuts, in a bowl, add the dressing and mix well. Divide among four large plates, then sprinkle with the macadamia nuts and a good grind of pepper and drizzle over any remaining dressing from the mixing bowl.

NOTE

To truss a chicken, you'll need about 40 cm (16 inches) of kitchen string. Place the bird on a chopping board, breast side up, with the legs facing you. Loop the centre of the string around the legs and pull them together, then take the string down and under the thighs, overlap it under the bird and then bring it up, catching the wings, to meet over the breast. Secure the string and cut off any excess. You are now ready to roast.

Fried eggs with spicy tamarind dressing

You can up the ante and use duck eggs in this dish, which are rich and delicious. I also like fried eggs with XO sauce or oyster sauce, or try nuoc cham dipping sauce as a dressing for a Vietnamese feel.

SERVES 1, OR 2 AS PART OF A SHARED BANQUET

+   To make the dressing, pound the chillies, garlic, coriander roots and sugar in a mortar with a pestle to a fine paste. Add the fish sauce, lime juice and tamarind water, then taste to check for balance.

+   Heat the oil in a wok or deep-fryer until just starting to smoke, about 180°C (350°F). Carefully crack the eggs into a bowl and then gently pour the whole eggs into the hot oil. Use a large spoon to ladle some of the hot oil over the top of the eggs until they are golden brown all over. Remove the eggs from the oil, drain on paper towel and transfer to a serving plate.

+   Allow the oil to cool a little, then fry one of the sliced shallots until golden and crisp. Remove with a slotted spoon and drain on paper towel.

+   Mix the herbs and both the fresh and fried shallots in a bowl and moisten with some of the dressing. Sprinkle the herb salad over the eggs, then drizzle with the remaining dressing to serve.

2 large free-range or organic eggs
vegetable oil, for deep-frying
2 French shallots, thinly sliced
1 small handful combined mint, coriander (cilantro) and Thai basil leaves

Dressing

1 long fresh red chilli, halved, seeded and chopped
3 wild green chillies (available from Asian grocers), chopped
1 garlic clove, chopped
2 coriander (cilantro) roots, scraped and chopped
1½ tablespoons caster (superfine) sugar
1½ tablespoons fish sauce
1½ tablespoons lime juice
1½ tablespoons tamarind water (see Note)

NOTE

To make tamarind water, break off 240 g (8½ oz) of tamarind pulp, soak in 375 ml (13 fl oz/1½ cups) boiling water for 20 minutes, mash and then push through a sieve.

Rigatoni with artichokes, anchovies and smoked bacon

Anchovies give an indescribable depth to your pasta dishes, spicing them up but without adding a fishy flavour. Obviously you could use any type of pasta you like here — macaroni, tagliatelle — it all works.

SERVES 4

+ Heat a large frying pan over low heat and add the olive oil and garlic, gently fry the garlic, without colouring, for 2 minutes. Add the anchovies, bacon and a pinch of sea salt and fry for 2 minutes. Add the onion and chilli flakes, and cook for about 10 minutes until the onion is soft and translucent and the anchovies have melted. Add the artichokes and lemon zest and cook for a further 3 minutes.

+ Meanwhile, cook the pasta in a large saucepan of heavily salted boiling water for about 8 minutes or until *al dente*. Drain the pasta, add to the sauce and toss through.

+ Add the lemon juice, parmesan, parsley and a grind of white pepper to the pasta and fold through. Spoon into four pasta bowls and serve immediately with your favourite bread.

4–6 cooked artichokes, halved or quartered if large and stems roughly sliced (see Note)
150 ml (5 fl oz) extra virgin olive oil
2 garlic cloves, thinly sliced
4 anchovy fillets
100 g (3½ oz) smoked bacon, roughly chopped
sea salt and freshly ground white pepper
½ small brown onion, thinly sliced
½ teaspoon chilli flakes
grated zest and juice of 1 lemon
400 g (14 oz) rigatoni
35 g (1¼ oz/⅓ cup) freshly grated parmesan
2 tablespoons chopped flat-leaf (Italian) parsley
bread, to serve

NOTE

To prepare fresh artichokes, trim the sharp points from the leaves, cut 2 cm (¾ inch) off the top of the choke, and trim the stems leaving about 2 cm attached. Use a teaspoon to remove the hairy centre. Place the trimmed artichokes in cold water with a squeeze of lemon juice. Bring to the boil, then simmer for 25 minutes until soft but still a touch firm.

Spaghetti with toasted breadcrumbs

This breadcrumb recipe is also good with a wide pasta such as fettuccine. Chilli adds great weight to the flavour of a dish. Dial it up or down depending on your love of heat.

SERVES 4

+   Preheat the oven to 200°C (400°F/Gas 6).

+   Place the breadcrumbs on a baking tray and toss with 60 ml (2 fl oz/¼ cup) olive oil and a little sea salt. Bake for 10–15 minutes or until golden.

+   Place the chilli, herbs, garlic, capers, anchovies, vinegar and remaining olive oil in a food processor and blend until smooth. Check the seasoning.

+   Cook the pasta in a large saucepan of salted boiling water for about 8 minutes or until *al dente*, then drain.

+   Place the pasta, herb mixture and three-quarters of the breadcrumbs in a large bowl and toss well. Divide among four pasta bowls and sprinkle with the remaining breadcrumbs. Give a good grind of white pepper and serve immediately.

400 g (14 oz) spaghetti
175 g (6 oz) fresh breadcrumbs
250 ml (9 fl oz/1 cup) extra virgin olive oil
sea salt and freshly ground white pepper
2–3 jalapeño chillies, halved lengthways and seeded
1 small bunch tarragon, leaves picked
2 handfuls flat-leaf (Italian) parsley leaves
1 garlic clove
2 tablespoons salted baby capers, well rinsed and drained
3 anchovy fillets
60 ml (2 fl oz/¼ cup) red wine vinegar

John Dory meunière

Lemon, butter and fish is a sublime combo, and this is a bona fide classic. Whiting, snapper and any mild-flavoured, white-fleshed fish is great here. I also like it with prawns, scallops and lobster.

SERVES 4

+ If you don't have a frying pan big enough to fit all four fillets, you will need to cook the fish in two batches, so warm the oven to 100°C (200°F/Gas ½) to keep the first batch warm and have a plate ready for the fish.

+ Place a large stainless-steel or non-stick frying pan over medium–high heat and pour in enough clarified butter to cover the base of the pan. Heat the butter until it is foaming.

+ Meanwhile, dip the fish fillets in the milk, then the flour, and sprinkle with sea salt. Place the fish fillets in the hot pan and cook for about 1 minute on each side or until golden. Remove from the pan and drain on absorbent paper towel. Reserve the pan.

+ Place a fish fillet on each of four plates, squeeze a little lemon juice over the fish, sprinkle with parsley and sea salt and give a good grind of white pepper.

+ Add the unsalted butter to the reserved pan and place over high heat. As the butter turns a nut-brown colour, spoon it over the fish. The butter, parsley and lemon juice will mingle to create the meunière sauce. Serve immediately.

4 John Dory fillets, about 200 g
(7 oz) each, skin off
clarified butter (see Notes)
125 ml (4 fl oz/½ cup) milk
150 g (5½ oz/1 cup) plain
(all-purpose) flour
sea salt and freshly ground
white pepper
2 lemons, quartered
2 tablespoons chopped flat-leaf
(Italian) parsley
125 g (4½ oz) unsalted butter,
cut into small cubes

NOTES

To make clarified butter, melt 250 g (9 oz) butter in a saucepan over medium heat, then strain off the milk solids and discard.

Serve the fish with boiled new potatoes tossed in butter or olive oil, and buttered peas (there's no shame in frozen).

Chopped tuna on rice

Raw tuna served this way is a fantastic meal and so good for you, but any super-fresh fish you like can be substituted. Bonito, mackerel and kingfish would be perfect.

SERVES 4

+ To make the dressing, place all the ingredients in a bowl and combine well.

+ Place the chopped tuna, spring onions, shiso, ginger, daikon and dressing in a stainless-steel bowl and mix to combine.

+ Divide the hot rice among four bowls, then top with the tuna mixture. Make a little well in each tuna mound and place a raw egg yolk in each one. Sprinkle with sesame seeds and serve. (Each person can then mix the tuna and yolk through the rice and eat with chopsticks or a spoon.)

NOTES

Korean hot bean paste is available from good Asian grocers or specialty stores. If you can't find it you can use any chilli paste, or just leave it out and increase the other ingredients.

Shiso leaves are available from good greengrocers or farmers' markets. If you can't find it, use Thai basil or mint or a combination of both.

The egg yolk can be omitted from the tuna dish, but the end result won't be quite so lush.

300 g (10½ oz) raw sashimi-quality tuna, finely chopped into 1 cm (½ inch) dice

4 spring onions (scallions), cut into rounds

10 purple or green shiso leaves, roughly chopped (see Note)

2 cm (¾ inch) knob of ginger, peeled and grated

4 cm (1½ inch) piece daikon, peeled and finely grated

260 g (9¼ oz/1¼ cups) short-grain sushi rice, cooked and kept hot

4 free-range egg yolks

½ teaspoon toasted white sesame seeds

Dressing

3 tablespoons *gochujang* (Korean hot bean paste) (see Note)

1 tablespoon caster (superfine) sugar

1 tablespoon rice wine vinegar

2 tablespoons soy sauce

1 teaspoon sesame oil

Barbecued snapper fillet with tomato sauce

This tomato sauce is a great all-rounder; it's delicious with any seafood or chicken, or even as a simple sauce for pasta.

SERVES 4

+ Preheat the barbecue grill plate to hot.

+ Grill the tomatoes for about 20 minutes, turning from time to time. They should colour and soften and the skin should blister and burn. Place them in a bowl and use tongs to remove as much of the skin as you can. Don't worry if little bits get left behind. Mash the flesh with a fork, then add the red wine vinegar, olive oil, herbs, sea salt and white pepper to taste and mix well.

+ Clean the grill. Sprinkle the fish with sea salt and brush with olive oil. Place the fish on the grill, skin side down, and cook for 3 minutes, then turn and cook for a further 2 minutes. Set aside to rest in a warm place for 3–4 minutes. The cooking time will vary depending on the thickness of your fillets so be careful. The fish should be just slightly firm to the touch, but still tender.

+ To serve, place a couple of generous tablespoons of tomato sauce on each plate and place the fish, skin side up, on top. Squeeze some lemon juice over the skin and finish with a sprinkle of sea salt and a grind of white pepper.

4 snapper fillets, about 200 g (7 oz) each, skin on
4 vine-ripened tomatoes, halved
60 ml (2 fl oz/¼ cup) good-quality red wine vinegar
150 ml (5 fl oz) extra virgin olive oil, plus extra, for brushing
2 tablespoons mixed soft herbs (such as tarragon, parsley, oregano), leaves only
sea salt and freshly ground white pepper
1 lemon

NOTES

The more you char the outside of the tomatoes, the more smoky the flavour they will have.

The fish is cooked longer on the skin side to make sure it is crisp. It is then turned just to seal the other side. Rest it and it will be perfectly cooked.

A fine skewer or opened-out paper clip will help you test if the fish is cooked. You should feel slight resistance when you push it into the flesh, and it will be perfect by the time it gets to the table.

Jewfish, mussel and saffron stew

You can use any firm-fleshed fish you like, such as salmon or monkfish tails, and clams are a fine stand-in for the mussels.

SERVES 8

8 jewfish steaks, about 200 g (7 oz) each, cut into thirds
2 kg (4 lb 8 oz) live green mussels, scrubbed and de-bearded
160 ml (5¼ fl oz) extra virgin olive oil
1 red onion, finely diced
4 garlic cloves
500 ml (17 fl oz/2 cups) white wine

1 teaspoon saffron threads, soaked in 60 ml (2 fl oz/¼ cup) hot water
sea salt and freshly ground white pepper
120 g (4¼ oz) unsalted butter, chopped
½ cup flat-leaf (Italian) parsley, finely shredded
crusty bread, to serve

+ Heat 80 ml (2½ fl oz/⅓ cup) of the olive oil in a large wide saucepan with a tight-fitting lid, which is large enough to fit the mussels, over medium heat. Add the onion and garlic and sauté for 5 minutes or until soft.

+ Increase the heat to high, then add the mussels, wine and saffron with its soaking liquid and cover with the lid. Cook, shaking frequently for 5 minutes or until the mussels begin to open. Remove from the heat and strain the mussels into a sieve placed over a bowl. If your pan isn't quite big enough to fit all the mussels comfortably, you may find you need to cook the mussels in two batches, which is fine. Simply scoop the first batch of cooked mussels out with a mesh strainer and keep aside while you cook the second batch. Strain the mussel broth through a fine sieve, leaving any gritty bits behind.

+ Season the fish with sea salt. Heat the remaining olive oil in a heavy-based, deep-sided frying pan over medium heat. Add the fish pieces and cook, without turning for 1 minute. Add the mussel broth and bring to a simmer. Cook the fish for a further 2 minutes, then turn over. Add the mussels and cook for 2 minutes or until the fish is just cooked.

+ Add the butter and gently stir through. Sprinkle the stew with the parsley and add a grind of white pepper.

+ To serve, place the pan on the table with a ladle and bowls for everyone, or serve in one beautiful big bowl to share among the guests. Serve with crusty bread on the side.

NOTE

For a spicy, Asian-style soup or stew, don't stop at saffron — add lemongrass, chilli, ginger and kaffir lime leaves.

Roast lobster

Absolutely nothing says 'I'm spoiling you' like this delicious lobster dish, so dive in and treat someone special.

SERVES 2

+ Preheat the oven to 200°C (400°F/Gas 6). Place the live lobster in the freezer for 1 hour (see Note).

+ Place the lobster on a chopping board, with its head towards you, and carefully place a sharp knife between its eyes. Now, holding the tail, cut down towards you, right through the shell. Turn the lobster around and, holding it by the head, cut through the tail; you should have two halves. Pull out the digestive tract that runs down its length.

+ Season the lobster halves with salt and place, cut side up in a roasting tin. Drizzle with a little olive oil and place slices of butter on each lobster half, from head to tail, so that all the meat is covered.

+ Roast for about 15 minutes, being very careful not to overcook the lobster. From time to time, spoon melted butter over the lobster flesh. When it is perfectly cooked, you should be able to just move the flesh away from the shell near the head. (The butter should be melted and even slightly burnt in the bottom of the roasting tin.) Place each lobster half on a large plate and reserve the roasting tin with its buttery juices.

+ Add the lemon juice, olive oil, parsley, a little sea salt and a good grind of white pepper to the butter in the roasting tin, and stir to combine well. Spoon the dressing over the lobsters and serve immediately, with lemon cheeks on the side.

1 live rock lobster, about 700–800 g (1 lb 9 oz–1 lb 12 oz), cleaned
sea salt and freshly ground white pepper
2 tablespoons extra virgin olive oil, plus extra, for drizzling
100 g (3½ oz) unsalted butter, thinly sliced
juice of 1 lemon
1 tablespoon chopped flat-leaf (Italian) parsley
lemon cheeks, to serve

NOTE

You can also kill a lobster by placing it in a pot of fresh water — the lobster goes to sleep and drowns.

Roast chicken with tofu and avocado salsa

This chicken dish is super quick if you buy a barbecued free-range chicken. If you have more time, barbecue or roast a quality bird yourself.

SERVES 4–6

+   To make the salsa, mash all the ingredients in a bowl, season to taste, then whisk until well combined.

+   Divide the lettuce among four plates. Combine the tomatoes, olive oil and lemon juice in a bowl and season to taste. Spoon the tomatoes over the lettuce, then top with the sliced chicken. Serve the salsa on the side or in generous dollops on the chicken.

NOTE

Keep the skin on the chicken. It's the best bit!

1.6 kg (3 lb 8 oz) free-range roast chicken (organic if possible), meat removed from the bones and sliced
1 iceberg lettuce heart, shredded
50 g (1¾ oz) cherry tomatoes, halved
60 ml (2 fl oz/¼ cup) extra virgin olive oil
juice of 1 lemon

Salsa

150 g (5½ oz) silken tofu
1 ripe avocado
100 g (3½ oz) fresh ricotta cheese
juice of 1 lemon
sea salt and freshly ground white pepper

Crumbed chicken breast with Moroccan eggplant and cumin mayonnaise

This combination of flavours is awesome — and so easy. The dish might not look all that attractive, but it sure tastes great served either warm or at room temperature. Make it once and this will be in your life forever.

SERVES 4

4 free-range skinless chicken breast fillets (organic if possible), about 120–150 g (4¼–5½ oz) each
150 g (5½ oz/1 cup) plain (all-purpose) flour, lightly seasoned
1 free-range egg, lightly beaten with 250 ml (9 fl oz/1 cup) milk, for egg wash
120 g (4¼ oz/2 cups) fresh breadcrumbs, made from day-old bread
100 ml (3½ fl oz) olive oil
80 g (2¾ oz) unsalted butter
sea salt and freshly ground pepper
lemon wedges, to serve

Moroccan eggplant

extra virgin olive oil
3 eggplants (aubergines), sliced into 1 cm (½ inch) rounds

1 handful flat-leaf (Italian) parsley leaves
4 vine-ripened tomatoes, peeled, seeded and diced
1 tablespoon ground cumin
sea salt and freshly ground white pepper
juice of 1 lemon

Cumin mayonnaise

150 ml (5½ fl oz) olive oil
2 teaspoons ground cumin
1 egg yolk, at room temperature
1 teaspoon dijon mustard
sea salt and freshly ground white pepper
lemon juice, to taste

+ To make the Moroccan eggplant, heat 1 cm (½ inch) olive oil in a large frying pan over medium–high heat until hot. Fry the eggplant, in three to four batches until brown all over. Remove to a bowl. Reduce the heat to low, then add the parsley to the hot oil (be careful as it will spit a fair bit). Add the tomato, cumin and sea salt to taste and toss for 1–2 minutes (don't burn the cumin). Add the eggplant and cook for a further 5 minutes. Add the lemon juice, check the seasoning and finish with a grind of white pepper. Set aside.

+ For the mayonnaise, place 50 ml (1¾ fl oz) of the olive oil and the cumin in a saucepan over low heat for 10 minutes to gently infuse. Remove from the heat, then cool to room temperature.

+ Place the egg yolk and mustard in a bowl, with a wet cloth underneath to stop it from slipping. Whisk until well combined. Whisking continuously, add the remaining oil, drop by drop at first, then in a slow, steady stream until emulsified. Whisk in the cumin infusion (leaving the cumin sediment behind), sea salt, white pepper and lemon juice to taste. Makes about 150 g (5½ oz).

+ Place each chicken fillet between two sheets of baking paper and gently beat with the side of a meat mallet (an empty wine bottle seems to work just as well at our house) just to even the thickness out a bit.

+ Set up a crumbing station with three bowls containing (from left to right) flour, egg wash and breadcrumbs. Coat 1 chicken fillet in flour and dust off the excess. Then dip in egg wash, then breadcrumbs, pressing to coat all over. Repeat with the remaining fillets, and set them aside.

+ Heat the olive oil and butter in a large non-stick frying pan over medium heat until foaming. Cook the chicken for about 5 minutes on one side or until the crumbs get a nice brown colour, then turn and cook the other side for a few minutes or until cooked through. Drain on paper towel.

+ Divide the Moroccan eggplant among four large plates, place a chicken fillet on each, covering half the eggplant, sprinkle with salt and a good grind of pepper, and add a dollop of cumin mayonnaise. Serve with lemon wedges.

NOTES

You can serve the eggplant and the cumin mayonnaise with anything you like. I love them with lamb or fish — the combo is particularly good with raw tuna.

If you don't want to crumb the chicken, just marinate it in cumin, lemon juice, olive oil and chopped coriander.

Stir-fried chicken with chilli sauce

Bring the unique flavours of Korea to your own kitchen — with or without the fiery chilli. This is great served with steamed rice or noodles and wonderful Asian salads.

SERVES 4 AS PART OF A SHARED BANQUET

+   For the sauce, place all the ingredients in a bowl and combine well.

+   Heat the oil in a wok over high heat until almost smoking. Add the chicken and brown it all over, then continue to stir-fry until it is almost cooked.

+   Add the chilli, onion, mushrooms and carrot, and cook for another minute. Add the sauce and bring to the boil.

+   To serve, spoon the chicken into a bowl and sprinkle with spring onion and sesame seeds.

200 g (7 oz) free-range chicken thigh fillets (organic if possible), sliced
2 tablespoons vegetable oil
3 fresh red chillies, thinly sliced into rounds
1 small brown onion, sliced
9 fresh shiitake mushrooms, stalks removed and caps thickly sliced
1 carrot, julienned
2 spring onions (scallions), finely chopped
1 teaspoon sesame seeds, toasted and coarsely crushed

Chilli sauce

3 tablespoons *gochujang* (Korean hot bean paste) (see Note page 22)
2 tablespoons red chilli powder (optional)
2 teaspoons light soy sauce
1 tablespoon crushed garlic
1 tablespoon finely chopped spring onion
1 teaspoon sugar
pinch of freshly ground black pepper
2 tablespoons sesame oil

Chicken and pickled ginger in honey sauce

If you like you can use Japanese pickled ginger in this chicken dish to add a further colour dimension.

SERVES 4

+ To make the marinade, combine all the ingredients in a bowl.

+ Add the chicken to the marinade, toss to combine well, then stand for 30 minutes.

+ Heat the peanut oil in a wok until it reaches 180°C (350°F) or until a cube of bread dropped into the oil turns golden brown in 15 seconds. Deep-fry the chicken in batches until lightly browned. Remove and drain on paper towel. Pour all but 2 teaspoons of the oil from the wok.

+ Reheat the wok over high heat until just smoking. Add the ginger and red and green capsicum and stir-fry for 30 seconds until fragrant. Deglaze the wok with the Shaoxing, then add the chicken, honey, soy sauce, salt and chicken stock. Cover and simmer over medium heat for 3 minutes, or until the chicken is cooked through. Serve with steamed rice.

NOTE

If you are worried about deep-frying, you can stir-fry the chicken. You'll need to cook it a little longer and you won't get the same texture on the skin, but you won't have to deal with lots of piping-hot oil smoking in a wok, either.

4 free-range chicken marylands (organic if possible), chopped through the bone into bite-sized pieces
1 litre (35 fl oz/4 cups) peanut oil, for deep-frying
125 g (4½ oz) Chinese pickled ginger, finely shredded
1 red capsicum (pepper), cut into large dice
1 green capsicum (pepper), cut into large dice
1 teaspoon Shaoxing rice wine
2 tablespoons honey
1 tablespoon dark soy sauce
1 teaspoon sea salt
125 ml (4 fl oz/½ cup) chicken stock
steamed rice, to serve

Marinade

1 tablespoon light soy sauce
1 teaspoon dark soy sauce
1 teaspoon Shaoxing rice wine
½ teaspoon salt

Sauté of chicken, garlic, olives, capers and red wine vinegar

This delicious chicken dish is silky and flavoursome. You can, of course, make it with skinless, boneless cuts, but the result is not nearly so enjoyable.

SERVES 4

8 large free-range chicken thighs (organic if possible), bone in and skin on
2 garlic bulbs, pulled apart, skins on
sea salt
extra virgin olive oil
2 bay leaves
2 thyme sprigs
12 black olives
1 teaspoon salted baby capers, rinsed and drained

2 vine-ripened tomatoes, peeled, seeded and diced
100 ml (3½ fl oz) good-quality red wine vinegar
40 g (1½ oz) unsalted butter
1 tablespoon flat-leaf (Italian) parsley, chopped
squeeze of lemon juice (optional)
freshly ground white pepper

+ Place the garlic cloves in a saucepan of cold water and bring to the boil. Drain and repeat. This makes the garlic mellow and sweet.

+ Season the chicken with salt. Drizzle a little olive oil in the base of a frying pan large enough to hold the chicken pieces in one layer. Place the pan over high heat and add the chicken, skin side down. Reduce the heat to medium, then add the garlic, bay leaves and thyme. Shake the pan to avoid sticking.

+ Cook the chicken for 10 minutes, moving the pan every few minutes so the garlic caramelises on all sides. Turn the chicken and cook for 8 minutes or until it is cooked through (large chicken pieces may take longer). Divide the chicken among four plates.

+ Add the olives, capers, tomatoes and vinegar to the pan, and simmer until the vinegar has almost gone. Add the butter and swirl the pan to make a sauce. Add the parsley, a squeeze of lemon, if desired, and a good grind of white pepper. Make sure you check the seasoning. Spoon the garlic, olives, capers and butter sauce over the chicken and serve.

NOTE

To take the chicken dish to the next level, buy a whole organic chook. Remove the legs and cut at the thigh and drumstick joint, remove the ribs and cage, take the wings off and split the breast. You'll end up with six wonderful pieces to cook.

Stir-fried beef with snow peas, black beans and chilli

These two wonderfully simple dishes will happily serve two, with rice. Add a whole steamed fish or a braised chicken dish and you have a feast for four.

SERVES 2

+ About 15 minutes before cooking, combine the marinade ingredients in a bowl. Add the beef and toss to coat well. Stand for 15 minutes.

+ Heat a wok over high heat until just smoking. Add the peanut oil and, when hot, fry the beef in batches until golden. Remove and drain on paper towel.

+ Pour all but 1 tablespoon of the oil from the wok, then reheat over high heat until just smoking. Add the ginger, spring onions and garlic and stir-fry until fragrant. Add the snow peas, chilli and black beans and cook for a further 30 seconds, then deglaze the wok with the Shaoxing or sherry.

+ Return the beef to the wok, then add the soy sauce, oyster sauce and chicken stock. Bring to the boil and combine well. Serve with steamed rice.

Stir-fried spinach with garlic

SERVES 2

+ Heat a wok over high heat until just smoking. Add the vegetable oil and, when hot, add the garlic and stir-fry until fragrant. Add the spinach and stir-fry for 3 minutes, or until it wilts. Moisture will come out of it, but don't worry.

+ Deglaze the wok with the Shaoxing or sherry, then add the soy sauce, sugar and salt and continue to cook for another 30 seconds until the spinach is tender. Remove from the heat and toss with the sesame oil to serve.

NOTES

Both dishes will welcome substitutes, so change the beef for chicken, lamb, pork, prawns or fish.

The spinach recipe works well, too, with choy sum (Chinese flowering cabbage), broccolini or any other green vegetable you love.

350 g (12 oz) beef fillet, thinly sliced across the grain, about 1 cm (½ inch) thick
250 ml (9 fl oz/1 cup) peanut oil
20 g (¾ oz) ginger, peeled and thinly sliced
3 spring onions (scallions), cut into 4 cm (1½ inch) lengths
1 garlic clove, crushed
10 snow peas (mangetout)
1 long fresh red chilli, sliced
1 tablespoon fermented black beans
1 teaspoon Shaoxing rice wine or dry sherry
1 tablespoon light soy sauce
1 tablespoon oyster sauce
60 ml (2 fl oz/¼ cup) chicken stock
steamed rice, to serve

Marinade

1 tablespoon light soy sauce
1 teaspoon sugar
1 tablespoon peanut oil

1 bunch English spinach (a little of the stems left on), washed well and dried
2 tablespoons vegetable oil
5 cloves garlic, smashed
1 tablespoon Shaoxing rice wine or dry sherry
1 tablespoon light soy sauce
1 teaspoon sugar
pinch of sea salt
1 teaspoon sesame oil

Classic pepper steak

This pepper steak dish is perfect with sautéed or boiled potatoes and boiled green beans. I also adore this steak with mushrooms — pan-roasted with garlic and herbs.

SERVES 4

+ Remove the steaks from the refrigerator 1 hour before cooking and season liberally with sea salt.

+ Roughly crush the peppercorns in a mortar and pestle and transfer to a plate. Press the steaks, one at a time, firmly onto the crushed peppercorns on both sides.

+ Place half the olive oil and half the butter into a heavy-based frying pan over medium heat. When hot, add 2 of the steaks and cook for 2 minutes. Turn the steaks and cook for another 2 minutes. Set aside in a warm place to rest. Repeat with the remaining oil, butter and steaks.

+ Add the brandy to the pan. As it flames, scrape the base of the pan with a wooden spoon to release all the flavours. When the flames have died down, add the cream and cook until reduced by half. Add a squeeze of lemon, check the seasoning and add a little more sea salt, if necessary.

+ Place the steaks on serving plates, pour over the pepper sauce and serve immediately.

NOTE

Place the meat between two pieces of baking paper and tap it out with a bottle or rolling pin until even and flat for a perfect minute steak.

4 Scotch fillet steaks, about 200 g (7 oz) each, lightly beaten to flatten (see Note)
sea salt
25 g (1 oz) mixed white and black peppercorns
60 ml (2 fl oz/¼ cup) extra virgin olive oil
40 g (1½ oz) unsalted butter
125 ml (4 fl oz/½ cup) brandy
500 ml (17 fl oz/2 cups) thin (pouring/whipping) cream
juice of 1 lemon

Beef on rice

This is a simple lesson in a perfect balance of Japanese flavours and makes for great one-bowl dining.

SERVES 4

+ Place the rice wine and 125 ml (4 fl oz/½ cup) water in a saucepan and bring to the boil over medium heat. Reduce the heat to low and simmer for 5 minutes. Add the soy sauce and mirin and simmer for a few more minutes.

+ Add the onion, capsicum and celery and simmer for 2–3 minutes, or until the vegetables have softened. Add the beef and simmer for 1 minute, stirring (the fillet will cook quickly).

+ Place the rice into four bowls. With a slotted spoon, place the beef and vegetables on top of the rice, then spoon as much broth over as you like. I like it quite soupy. Top the beef with a little pickled ginger and coriander, if using, and serve.

600 g (1 lb 5 oz) beef fillet,
  thinly sliced
250 ml (9 fl oz/1 cup) rice wine
125 ml (4 fl oz/½ cup) soy sauce
250 ml (9 fl oz/1 cup) mirin
2 white onions, peeled, halved
  and sliced into 1 cm (½ inch) slices
1 red capsicum (pepper), quartered,
  seeds removed, and flesh cut into
  1 cm (½ inch) batons
2 celery stalks, cut on the diagonal
  into 1 cm (½ inch) slices
210 g (7½ oz/1 cup) sushi rice, cooked
  and kept warm (see Note)
pickled ginger and coriander
  (cilantro) leaves (optional), to serve

NOTES

Short-grain rice, which is used in Japanese and Korean cookery, is starchier than long- and medium-grain rice, and makes a very comforting base for one-bowl meals like this one.

If your budget doesn't stretch to beef fillet, use thinly cut chuck steak. Just boil it in water for 5 minutes, rinse it and add it to the broth, simmering gently for about 10 minutes before you add the vegetables.

Grilled aged rib-eye with tomato, onion and chipotle salsa

A hint of chilli turns a simple steak into a meal fit for a king. I adore the smokiness of this salsa.

SERVES 4

+ Preheat the oven to 200°C (400°F/Gas 6).

+ Season the steaks well with sea salt up to 2 hours before cooking, and allow them to come to room temperature.

+ To make the salsa, place the tomatoes and onion in a small ovenproof dish (that holds the tomatoes snugly), pour the olive oil over and season with sea salt. Roast for 1 hour or until the skins of the tomatoes burn a little.

+ Remove from the oven, pull off the tomato skins, then place the contents of the dish in a small saucepan and mash the tomatoes with a pair of tongs. You should have a sauce with lots of olive oil on top. Bring it to the boil (the oil will then blend in), reduce it by a third, then add the chipotle powder and mix through. Cook for a further minute, then remove from the heat and allow to cool. Add the parsley and lime juice, then season to taste with sea salt and white pepper. Makes about 250 g (9 oz/1 cup).

+ Heat a flat or ridged chargrill pan on the stovetop or heat the barbecue to very hot.

+ Rub the steaks with a little olive oil. Cook them for about 2 minutes (for rare), then turn over and cook for a further 2 minutes. Allow the meat to rest in a warm place for 5 minutes.

+ Place the steaks on serving plates, top with a dollop of room-temperature salsa and drizzle with extra virgin olive oil. Serve with your favourite potatoes and a bowl of boiled greens.

4 grass-fed rib-eye steaks with bone in, about 360 g (12¾ oz) each
sea salt
extra virgin olive oil, for drizzling

Salsa

4 large vine-ripened tomatoes
1 small red onion, thinly sliced
100 ml (3½ fl oz) extra virgin olive oil
sea salt and freshly ground white pepper
1½ tablespoons chipotle chilli powder, or to taste
1 tablespoon roughly chopped flat-leaf (Italian) parsley
juice of 1 lime

NOTES

Go to a good butcher and buy a quality rib-eye steak. It is the hero, so the effort will be worth it at the dinner table.

Chipotle chillies are jalapeños that have been dried and smoked. Ground, they are a wonderful addition to all sorts of dressings and sauces.

Roast duck with poached pears

This twice-cooked method gives a crisp, tasty duck that is well done and melts in the mouth. I also love to use quinces or figs here.

SERVES 4

+ To prepare the pears, peel then slice them lengthways into quarters; do not remove the core. Place the pears and peelings in a large heavy-based saucepan. Add 500 ml (17 fl oz/2 cups) water and all the remaining ingredients except the lemon juice and bring slowly to the boil over medium–high heat.

+ Reduce the heat to low and cook slowly for about 30–35 minutes or until the pears are soft, yet slightly firm. They should turn a lovely red colour.

+ Remove the pan from the heat and leave the pears to cool in the liquid. When cool, lift out the pears with a slotted spoon. Remove the core before serving, if you wish.

+ Place one duck on a chopping board and remove the fat deposits from the cavity. Cut off the neck and remove the wing tips at the second joint. Season the duck inside and out with sea salt. Repeat with the second duck.

+ Steam the ducks in a large steamer over boiling water for 45 minutes; be careful not to let the saucepan boil dry. (You can also use two stacked bamboo steamers, swapping top and bottom halfway through steaming, or cook them one at a time in a small steamer.)

+ When the ducks are cool enough to handle, place one on a board and remove the legs. Cut down each side of the backbone and remove it. Remove the breasts, leaving them on the bone. Repeat with the other duck. You now have four breast pieces and four legs.

+ Preheat the oven to 220°C (425°F/Gas 7).

+ Rub the duck pieces with olive oil and season with sea salt. Place in a roasting tin in a single layer, skin side down, and cook for 15 minutes, then turn over. Pour off any excess liquid and cook for a further 15–20 minutes. The duck should be cooked and the skin crisp.

+ Cut the legs in half at the joint, remove the breast from the bone and carve it into slices.

+ To serve, place a whole duck leg on each of four plates and drape slices of breast over. Place slices of poached pear next to the duck. Drizzle the duck with olive oil and balsamic vinegar and add a sprinkle of sea salt and a grind of white pepper. Serve with sautéed peas and smoked bacon (see Notes) on the side, if desired.

2 x 2 kg (4 lb 8 oz) whole ducks
sea salt and freshly ground
 white pepper
extra virgin olive oil, for rubbing
aged balsamic vinegar, for drizzling

Poached pears

2 large pears
600 g (1 lb 5 oz) caster (superfine)
 sugar
500 ml (17 fl oz/2 cups) good-quality
 red wine
1 piece cassia bark (you can also
 use 1 cinnamon stick)
2 cloves
grated zest of 1 orange

NOTES

Any fresh green vegetable, boiled and drizzled with olive oil and lemon, is fantastic with this roast duck.

I like to sauté frozen peas with onion and garlic, and then add a little water — it is so easy and the peas are so sweet. For a special treat, add smoked bacon to the peas and you will be hooked forever.

Do a big batch of the pears and keep them in the refrigerator. They are great with muesli, yoghurt and honey for breakfast.

You can also strain the poaching liquid, reduce it to syrup consistency and serve it with the pears, if desired. If it is too sweet, adjust the taste with a little lemon juice.

Barbecued T-bone steak with anchovy butter

For a great barbecue, serve the steak with a couple of simple salads. Any cut of meat good for grilling works here, and most are great with the anchovy butter. It is the natural saltiness that works so well with the crust of the beef.

SERVES 4

4 grass-fed T-bone steaks, about 500 g
  (1 lb 2 oz) each
1 small handful oregano leaves
1 rosemary sprig, leaves picked
6 sage leaves
extra virgin olive oil, for drizzling
sea salt and freshly ground white pepper
lemon wedges, to serve

Anchovy butter
125 g (4½ oz) anchovy fillets
250 g (9 oz) unsalted butter,
  at room temperature
juice of ½ lemon
freshly ground white pepper,
  to taste

+ Remove the steaks from the refrigerator 1 hour before cooking.

+ To make the anchovy butter, place the butter and anchovies in a food processor and purée. Add the lemon juice and white pepper to taste and process for a further minute. Roll the mixture in a sheet of baking paper or foil into a log shape about 35 cm (14 inches) long and 4 cm (1½ inches) in diameter. Wrap in plastic wrap and refrigerate until firm.

+ To prepare the meat, roughly chop the herbs and press them onto both sides of the steaks.

+ Heat a chargrill pan or barbecue until smoking. Drizzle the steaks with olive oil and sprinkle with sea salt. Cook for about 6 minutes on one side and 4 minutes on the other, for medium-rare, or cook to your liking. Remove and place in a warm oven for 10 minutes.

+ To serve, place the steaks onto four dinner plates and top each with a 1 cm (½ inch) thick slice of anchovy butter. Pour over any resting juices from the steaks, then drizzle with extra virgin olive oil, plenty of white pepper and a sprinkle of sea salt. Serve with lemon wedges.

NOTE

Although the anchovy butter will make much more than you need (about 35 serves) it freezes well for up to 6 months. It's addictively good dolloped on a roast or on fish. You can slice portions off frozen, then bring to room temperature to soften slightly before adding to the meat.

Spiced pork braised with prunes and apricots

This is a rich, spicy pork braise but chicken or diced lamb shoulder will also complement the fruit in the braise. Instead of prunes and apricots, you could use other dried fruit such as dates, and add nuts like almonds.

SERVES 4

+ Mix the spices and salt in a small bowl, then rub over the pork, cover with plastic wrap and set aside to marinate for 1 hour.

+ Heat the olive oil in a large heavy-based saucepan with a tight-fitting lid over medium–high heat. When hot, fry half the pork until evenly browned, taking care not to burn the spices, then set aside. Repeat with the remaining pork. Set all the meat aside.

+ Add the onion to the pan with a little extra salt and cook over medium heat for 5 minutes or until soft. Add the port and simmer until reduced by half. Add the wine and simmer for 5 minutes to burn off the alcohol.

+ Return the pork to the pan, then add the prunes, apricots, orange zest, bay leaves and veal stock and bring to the boil. Reduce the heat to low, cover and cook for 1½ hours. Remove the lid and cook for a further 20–30 minutes, or until the pork is tender.

+ Remove the bay leaves and divide the braised pork among four serving bowls. Top with a good grind of white pepper and serve with soft polenta or rice.

1 kg (2 lb 4 oz) pork shoulder, cut into 2 cm (¾ inch) dice
1 teaspoon ground coriander
1 teaspoon ground fennel
1 teaspoon ground cumin
1 teaspoon ground cinnamon
2 teaspoons sea salt, plus extra
80 ml (2½ fl oz/⅓ cup) extra virgin olive oil
1 brown onion, cut into 2 cm (¾ inch) dice
125 ml (4 fl oz/½ cup) port
250 ml (9 fl oz/1 cup) red wine
8 pitted prunes
8 dried apricots
grated zest of 1 orange
2 bay leaves, fresh or dried
500 ml (9 fl oz/2 cups) veal stock
freshly ground white pepper
soft polenta (see page 180) or steamed rice, to serve

Fresh peaches
with zabaglione

I love zabaglione with any fruit. You don't have to peel the peaches, but it is a nice touch and the texture is more pleasing.

SERVES 4

+ Bring a saucepan of water to the boil. Make a crisscross cut in the base of each peach. Place the peaches in the boiling water for 10 seconds, remove and place in iced water. You should now be able to remove the skin easily. Reduce the heat to low so that the boiling water is at a gentle simmer.

+ Place the egg yolks and sugar in a bowl that will rest easily on top of the saucepan. Using a hand-held electric beater, whisk the yolks and sugar until they are thick and pale. Place the bowl over the saucepan of gently simmering water (it must not touch the water). Add the Marsala to the yolk mix, and beat continuously for at least 15 minutes or until the mixture forms soft peaks. This can be done by hand with a whisk, if you wish.

+ Spoon the zabaglione into four bowls, then top with the peaches. You can also sprinkle almond slivers over the top, if desired; they make a welcome crunchy addition.

NOTE

The zabaglione is great with fruit salad and I also love it made with a light sweet wine like moscato instead of the Marsala.

4 ripe peaches (slip-stone are best)
4 free-range or organic egg yolks
60 g (2¼ oz) caster (superfine) sugar
80 ml (2½ fl oz/⅓ cup) dry
   Marsala (wine)
toasted slivered almonds,
   to serve (optional)

Easy apple tart

This apple tart is super quick and can be easily adapted to other fruit. I like it served hot straight from the oven.

SERVES 8–10

+ Preheat the oven to 220°C (425°F/Gas 7). Place a heavy-based baking tray in the oven to preheat.

+ Roll the pastry out to 5 mm (¼ inch) thick. Cut out a 30 cm (12 inch) diameter circle using a dinner plate or flan ring as a guide, then place the pastry disc on a piece of baking paper.

+ Slice the apple into 2 mm (¹⁄₁₆ inch) slices, discarding the ends so you have good slices of apple. Place overlapping apple slices along the outside edge of the pastry. Continue with another smaller circle, overlapping, just inside the first, then finish with a few in the middle, so the pastry is covered with apple. Sprinkle with the sugar and dot with the chopped butter. Place the tart on the hot baking tray and place in the oven.

+ Bake for 20–30 minutes or until golden and the pastry is cooked. Serve warm or slide the tart onto a cake rack to cool. Cut the tart into wedges and serve with whipped cream or ice cream.

NOTE

Don't worry if the caramel dribbles onto the baking tray — as long as it doesn't burn too badly, it adds character and crispness.

6 granny smith apples, peeled, cored and halved
200 g (7 oz) block store-bought puff pastry
75 g (2¾ oz/⅓ cup) sugar
40 g (1½ oz) unsalted butter, chopped
whipped cream or ice cream, to serve (optional)

Strawberry mess

Mascarpone lightened with whipped egg whites and sugar can be substituted for the cream to make a rich, delicious mess.

SERVES 6

+ To make the meringues, preheat the oven to 160°C (315°F/ Gas 2–3). Line a large baking tray with baking paper.

+ Using an electric mixer, whisk the egg whites in a clean bowl until stiff peaks form, then add the sugar, one tablespoon at a time, then the vanilla and continue beating for about 5 minutes or until the meringue is shiny. Place the mixture in a piping (icing) bag fitted with a 5 mm (¼ inch) nozzle and pipe 2 cm (¾ inch) rounds onto the baking tray, leaving room between the meringues, as they will spread and puff. Place the tray in the oven, turn the temperature down to 120°C (235°F/Gas ½) and bake for about 30 minutes. Remove from the oven, cool completely, then store in an airtight container until ready to serve.

+ Meanwhile, to make the strawberry coulis, place the strawberries, sugar and lemon juice in a blender and purée until smooth. Push through a sieve, discard the seeds and set aside.

+ To serve, whip the cream until it will just about keep its shape, then place a dollop in the base of six nice glasses. Add some meringues, a drizzle of coulis and some strawberries. Repeat the process and you have a lovely layered dessert ready to serve. I also like to layer this into one large beautiful glass or bowl and serve from there — it's such a great looking dessert.

500 g (1 lb 2 oz) strawberries, hulled and quartered
300 ml (10½ fl oz) thin (pouring/ whipping) cream

Meringues

2 free-range egg whites
120 g (4¼ oz) caster (superfine) sugar
2 drops natural vanilla extract

Strawberry coulis

250 g (9 oz) strawberries, hulled
2 teaspoons caster (superfine) sugar
squeeze of lemon juice

NOTES

If you don't want to pipe the meringues, just dollop teaspoonfuls onto the baking paper.

Store any leftover meringues in an airtight jar and serve with your favourite citrus curd or stick together with chocolate ganache for a fast, sweet treat.

Coffee ice cream

This is awesome by itself but also goes brilliantly with anything chocolate or caramel.

SERVES 8–12

+ Whisk the egg yolks and sugar together until pale and creamy.

+ Place the milk and ground coffee in a saucepan and place over low heat until it just comes to the boil. Remove from the heat and stand for 10 minutes to allow the flavours to infuse. Strain through a fine sieve, then, whisking continuously, pour the coffee-flavoured milk into the egg mixture and combine well.

+ Place the mixture in a heavy-based saucepan and cook the custard to 85°C (185°F) or until it coats the back of a spoon (be careful not to scramble the eggs). Pour through a sieve into a bowl and set over ice to cool. When it is cold add the cream and churn in an ice-cream machine according to the manufacturer's instructions.

9 free-range egg yolks
200 g (7 oz) caster (superfine) sugar
500 ml (17 fl oz/2 cups) milk
125 g (4½ oz) ground coffee
300 ml (10½ fl oz) thin (pouring/whipping) cream (35% butterfat)

Candied almonds

I love these candied almonds for a fantastic crunch — it is a great texture with the silkiness of ice cream.

SERVES 8–12

+ Preheat the oven to 180°C (350°F/Gas 4). Line a baking tray with non-stick baking paper. Roast the almonds 10–12 minutes or until lightly golden. Remove from the oven, roughly chop and then keep the chopped almonds warm in the oven on low heat.

+ Combine the glucose, caster sugar and 2 tablespoons water in a small saucepan. Stir over a medium–low heat till the sugar has dissolved, then increase the heat and bring to the boil. Without stirring, continue to boil the sugar and allow it to caramelise. As the sugar starts to turn golden, lower the heat and cook until it turns a dark amber colour.

+ Remove the saucepan from the heat and quickly stir in the roasted almonds. Pour the mixture into a thin layer on a lightly greased baking tray, and set aside to cool. When cool, Break into pieces and roughly chop or process until finely chopped. Store in an airtight container.

120 g (4¼ oz/¾ cup) almonds
120 g (4¼ oz) glucose syrup
150 g (5½ oz) caster (superfine) sugar

Cherry clafoutis

The clafoutis is a classic. Cherries baked in batter and served at the table. Make sure you have a pretty ovenproof dish as it is great to drop the clafoutis in the middle of the table and serve from there.

SERVES 6

+ Preheat the oven to 180°C (350°F/Gas 4). Lightly brush a 2 litre (70 fl oz/8 cup) ovenproof dish with a little of the butter and scatter the cherries over the base.

+ Place the eggs, flour and caster sugar in a bowl and whisk until smooth. Gradually whisk in the cooled melted butter and the milk. Pour the batter over the cherries and bake for 30–35 minutes or until golden and puffed. Dust with icing sugar and stand for a few minutes before serving with a dollop of whipped cream.

500 g (1 lb 2 oz) pitted fresh cherries
80 g (2¾ oz) unsalted butter, melted and cooled
2 free-range eggs, lightly beaten
75 g (2¾ oz/½ cup) plain (all-purpose) flour
75 g (2¾ oz/⅓ cup) caster (superfine) sugar
170 ml (5½ fl oz/⅔ cup) milk
icing (confectioners') sugar, for dusting
whipped thick (double/heavy) cream, to serve

NOTE

Of course, simply pitted with vanilla bean ice cream is a fab way to eat cherries, and don't be afraid to pickle a few jars so you can serve them with pork and duck in the winter months.

Asian banquet

This is a terrific banquet for a special occasion as it is so simple to put together — you'll be feasting with friends and family instead of being stuck in the kitchen. Make the salad, braise the chicken so it's ready to reheat, place the fish in the steamer. Instead of prawns in the salad, you could use a roast chicken — just remove the skin and shred the meat.

MENU SERVES 8

Classic red braised chicken

This dish is called red braised because of the reddish-brown colour the sauce goes with the sugar and soy. Red braising differs from master stocking in that the cooking stock becomes the sauce and isn't saved for later cooking. You can easily substitute pork, duck or beef in this dish.

+ Combine the chicken, rice wine, garlic, ginger and spring onion in a bowl, cover with plastic wrap and leave to marinate for 30 minutes. Drain and reserve the marinade. Pat the chicken dry with paper towel.

+ Heat a wok over high heat until smoking. Add the peanut oil and, when hot, add the chicken and stir-fry for about 5 minutes until nicely brown. Add the reserved marinade and cook for a minute, then add all the remaining ingredients and 1.5 litres (52 fl oz/6 cups) water. Cover the wok, bring to the boil, reduce the heat to low and simmer gently for about 20 minutes or until the chicken is tender.

+ Using a slotted spoon, spoon the chicken and all the aromatics into a bowl. Return the sauce to the heat and boil for about 5 minutes until it thickens, then pour it over the chicken and serve.

8–12 free-range chicken drumsticks (organic if possible) cut into 3 cm (1¼ inch) pieces across the bone
500 ml (17 fl oz/2 cups) Shaoxing rice wine
6 garlic cloves, thinly sliced
4 cm (1½ inch) knob of ginger, peeled and thinly sliced
4 spring onions (scallions), cut into 2 cm (¾ inch) lengths
125 ml (4 fl oz/½ cup) peanut oil
125 ml (4 fl oz/½ cup) dark soy sauce
8 star anise
6 cinnamon sticks
4 pieces dried tangerine peel, soaked in hot water for 1 hour, then drained
2 small dried red chillies
160 g (5¾ oz/½ cup) crushed yellow rock sugar (available from Asian grocers)

Spicy prawn and tofu salad

+ To make the dressing, pound the chillies, shallots and sea salt in a mortar until a paste forms. Add the peanuts and continue to pound until smooth. Add the sugar, fish sauce, tamarind water and 80 ml (2½ fl oz/⅓ cup) water, combine well and check that the flavours are balanced.

+ Place the prawns, tofu, cucumber, carrot, bean sprouts and peanuts in a serving bowl, then add the dressing and toss.

16 cooked king prawns (shrimp), peeled, deveined and halved lengthways
300 g (10½ oz) marinated pressed tofu (available from supermarkets and Asian grocers), thinly sliced
2 small Lebanese (short) cucumbers, halved, seeded and julienned
1 large carrot, julienned
200 g (7 oz/1⅔ cup) bean sprouts, trimmed
50 g (1¾ fl oz/⅓ cup) roasted peanuts, crushed

Dressing
6 long fresh red chillies, seeded and chopped
2 red Asian shallots, chopped
pinch of sea salt
50 g (1¾ oz/⅓ cup) roasted peanuts
75 g (2¾ oz/⅓ cup) caster (superfine) sugar
50 ml (1¾ fl oz) fish sauce
80 ml (2½ fl oz/⅓ cup) tamarind water (see Note page 13)

Steamed whole snapper and mustard greens with black beans and chilli

+ Score the fish with diagonal lines, nearly to the bone on both sides. Divide the spring onions and mustard greens between two large, shallow heatproof bowls and place a snapper on top of each.

+ Combine the black beans, chilli, soy sauce, sugar, sesame oil and rice wine and pour over the fish. Place each bowl in a large steamer over a saucepan (or wok) of rapidly boiling water, cover with the lids and steam for 10 minutes or until the fish is just cooked through. Carefully remove the bowls from the steamers.

+ Heat the peanut oil in a small saucepan until just smoking and douse the fish with the hot oil just before serving.

2 whole snapper (about 1 kg/ 2 lb 4 oz each), cleaned
4 spring onions (scallions), trimmed and halved
1 cup roughly chopped salted mustard greens, well rinsed and hard stems removed
40 g (1½ oz/⅓ cup) fermented black beans, roughly chopped
2 long fresh red chillies, sliced on the diagonal and seeds left in
2 tablespoons light soy sauce
2 teaspoons sugar
½ teaspoon sesame oil
1 tablespoon Shaoxing rice wine
125 ml (4 fl oz/½ cup) peanut oil

Mangoes with black sticky rice and coconut cream

This is such a great dessert and it must be made at least once during mango season. Once you have prepared it you will see how easy it is. I love it with bananas too, but don't discount other fruit like figs and custard apples, all wonderful with the unctuous texture of the rice.

SERVES 8

500 g (1 lb 2 oz/2½ cups) black sticky rice
1 pandanus leaf, tied in a knot
180 g (6¼ oz/1 cup) chopped dark
  Indonesian palm sugar (jaggery)

430 ml (15 fl oz) coconut milk
125 ml (4 fl oz/½ cup) Kara coconut
  cream (see Note)
2 ripe mangoes, peeled and sliced

+ Rinse the rice under cold running water and place into a saucepan with the pandanus leaf and 1 litre (35 fl oz/4 cups) of water. Bring to the boil, then reduce the heat to low and simmer gently for 25 minutes, or until all the water has been absorbed. Remove from the heat and cover the pan with foil or a lid. Set aside and allow the rice to steam through for about 10 minutes or until tender. Remove the pandanus leaf.

+ Meanwhile, place the palm sugar and 125 ml (4 fl oz/½ cup) water in a small saucepan and stir over low heat until the sugar has dissolved. Bring to the boil, then simmer until a light syrup forms. Remove from the heat.

+ Return the pan of rice to low heat. Gradually add the coconut milk and most of the palm sugar syrup, stirring until heated through.

+ Divide the sticky rice between eight serving bowls, then top with the sliced mango. Drizzle with the coconut cream and remaining palm sugar syrup and serve.

NOTE

Kara cream is stabilised so it won't split; available readily, it is great for desserts and is perfect for when you want a creamy texture.

Saturday

Prosciutto and green bean salad with eggplant caviar

This eggplant caviar is great on bruschetta as a canapé, or try pan-frying or barbecuing a nice piece of firm, white-fleshed fish and serving the eggplant caviar as a salsa on the top or the side.

SERVES 4

+ To make the eggplant caviar, peel and cut the eggplant into 5 mm (¼ inch) dice. Place the eggplant immediately into a bowl with 500 ml (17 fl oz/2 cups) water and half the lemon juice. This stops the eggplant from browning and keeps it nice and white. Drain the eggplant, squeeze out the excess water, then steam it for 10 minutes, or until just tender, then place into a bowl.

+ Heat 3 teaspoons of the olive oil in a heavy-based saucepan over low heat. Add the onion, garlic and a pinch of salt and cook for 3 minutes or until the onion is very soft. Add the eggplant with the remaining oil, lemon juice, tarragon and tomato and season to taste.

+ Cook the beans in salted boiling water for 6 minutes, then drain and refresh in iced water. Drain again, then place in a bowl. Dress the beans with the lemon juice and a little olive oil, and season to taste.

+ Divide the prosciutto and beans among four plates. Top the beans with the eggplant caviar, drizzle with more oil, season with a good grind of pepper and sea salt and sprinkle with chives, then serve with thin slices of sourdough toast.

16 slices good-quality prosciutto
200 g (7 oz) baby green beans, trimmed
juice of 1 lemon
125 ml (4 fl oz/½ cup) extra virgin olive oil
sea salt and freshly ground white pepper
½ bunch chives, very thinly sliced
sourdough toast, to serve

Eggplant caviar

1 small eggplant (aubergine)
juice of 2 lemons
1½ tablespoons extra virgin olive oil
½ red onion, finely diced
2 garlic cloves, crushed
sea salt and freshly ground white pepper
10 French tarragon leaves, roughly chopped
1 ripe tomato, peeled, seeded and finely diced

Chopped raw beef with jalapeño salad and bruschetta

This crudo or raw beef is inspired by a wonderful dish I had at my favourite Italian restaurant, The River Café in London. Being a chilli nut I have added jalapeño to the salad. As you mix the meat and salad and eat it with bruschetta you get a really fresh hot hit from the chilli. Sorry, I couldn't help it, but by all means leave it out.

SERVES 6

+ Clean any fat or sinew off the beef. Place it on a chopping board and, using a very sharp large knife, slice it as thinly as possible, then slice it crossways in a thin julienne.

+ Now chop the meat until you have a nice fine texture — don't go too crazy, we're not looking for a paste. Place in a bowl and season with sea salt and white pepper. Add the lemon juice, stir in the olive oil and mix well.

+ For the salad, place the radicchio, chilli and lemon juice in a bowl, drizzle with the olive oil and season to taste with salt. Gently toss, then place on one side of each of the six serving plates. Divide the beef among the plates, then sprinkle with grated parmesan and give a good grind of pepper. Grill (broil) the sourdough, drizzle with extra olive oil and serve immediately with the chopped raw beef and extra lemon.

500 g (1 lb 2 oz) high-quality
   beef fillet
sea salt and freshly ground
   white pepper
2 lemons, 1 juiced, 1 cut
   into wedges
150 ml (5 fl oz) extra virgin olive oil,
   plus extra, for drizzling
freshly grated parmesan, to serve
6 pieces of really nice
   sourdough bread

Salad

1 small, tight radicchio heart,
   washed, dried and shredded
2 small jalapeño chillies, halved
   lengthways, seeded and
   finely chopped
1 tablespoon lemon juice
60 ml (2 fl oz/¼ cup) extra virgin
   olive oil

NOTE

Please use hunks of Italian parmesan (as if there is any other) and grate freshly over the beef. If you are going to buy that horrible grated stuff then cook another dish and leave this jewel alone!

King prawn, nectarine and feta salad

Don't let the nectarine season go by without showcasing them in this lovely prawn salad.

SERVES 4

+ For the dressing, place all the ingredients in a small jar, seal and shake together. Check the seasoning and adjust if necessary.

+ Using a sharp knife, cut the prawns in half lengthways.

+ In a bowl, place the treviso, baby cos and red onion and half the dressing. Divide the leaf mix among four bowls, then scatter the prawns and the nectarine slices over the top. Crumble the feta on top, sprinkle with the crushed hazelnuts and season with a little sea salt and a good grind of white pepper. Drizzle the remaining dressing over the salads and serve immediately.

NOTES

Don't let the absence of nectarines slow you down with variations on this salad. Peaches are great, as are most stone fruits, but things like ripe pear and even fig would be awesome as well. Almonds would happily substitute for the hazelnuts and just add almond oil instead of hazelnut.

It may sound crazy but I do like the prawns with blue cheese and pears but if you think that is too much, leave the prawns out and have a wonderful pear, blue cheese and nut salad.

12 large cooked king prawns (shrimp), peeled and deveined
2 heads treviso or red witlof, leaves separated, washed and dried
1 baby cos (romaine) lettuce, leaves separated, washed and dried
½ small red onion, thinly sliced
2 ripe nectarines, cut into circular slices
100 g (3½ oz) good-quality feta
75 g (2¾ oz/½ cup) roasted hazelnuts, peeled and lightly crushed
sea salt and freshly ground white pepper

Dressing

60 ml (2½ fl oz/¼ cup) extra virgin olive oil
1 tablespoon hazelnut oil (optional)
juice of 1 lemon
sea salt and freshly ground white pepper

Deep-fried zucchini flowers

SERVES 4

+ To prepare the zucchini flowers, remove the stamens from the centre and the green sepals from the base of each flower. Keep the stalks attached.

+ Fill a large saucepan or deep-fryer two-thirds full of oil or to the fill line. Heat the oil to 180°C (350°F) — use a thermometer if you are using a saucepan.

+ Pour the beer into a bowl, then sift in enough flour to make a batter with the same consistency as pouring cream. Only don't mix it with a whisk — use a chopstick. It is good not fully incorporated, leave the odd lump, season with sea salt and freshly ground white pepper. Now add the ice cubes.

+ Sift the flour for dusting onto a plate and place it next to the batter and hot oil.

+ Working in batches, hold the flowers by the stalks and dust in the flour, then dip into the batter. Tap off any excess batter on the side of the bowl and place them, one at a time, into the hot oil. Turn the flowers in the oil until they become golden and crisp. Drain on paper towel, then sprinkle with sea salt and freshly ground white pepper and serve immediately with lemon wedges.

12 male zucchini (courgette) flowers (see Notes)
vegetable oil, for deep-frying
375 ml (13 fl oz/1½ cup) can cold beer
150 g (5½ oz) plain (all-purpose) flour, approximately, plus extra flour, for dusting
sea salt and freshly ground white pepper
12 ice cubes
lemon wedges, to serve

NOTES

Male flowers have the stem and female have the fruit attached, You can use either but I like the crunchy light flowers for this very simple dish.

By all means stuff the zucchini flowers if you wish with fresh ricotta cheese or a mixture of cheeses. Just make and season the mix and pipe into the flower, closing it round the cheese, then continue with the batter and fry part of the method.

Warm Korean-style beef noodle salad

This dish would be great to add to some of the other Korean dishes I have peppered through this book to make a banquet.

SERVES 4 AS PART OF A SHARED BANQUET

120 g (4¼ oz) beef fillet, sinew trimmed and cut into thin strips
2 tablespoons soy sauce
2 tablespoons sugar
2 tablespoons sesame oil
1 tablespoon vegetable oil
4 dried Chinese mushrooms, soaked for 30 minutes in several changes of water, squeezed out and sliced
1 small white onion, sliced

sea salt
1 carrot, cut into julienne
½ bunch English spinach, washed, blanched in boiling water for 1 minute and refreshed
120 g (4¼ oz) dried soba noodles, cooked in boiling water until tender, then refreshed in iced water
1 teaspoon sesame seeds, toasted
1 teaspoon pine nuts, toasted and crushed

+ Place the beef in a bowl with half the soy sauce, sugar and sesame oil. Toss to coat well, then leave to marinate for 20 minutes.

+ Heat the vegetable oil in a wok over high heat until almost smoking. Add the beef and sliced mushrooms and stir-fry for about 4 minutes until both are well cooked. Set aside in a bowl.

+ Add the onion and a pinch of sea salt to the hot wok and stir-fry for 1 minute until soft and coloured. Add the carrot and cook for a further minute, then add the spinach and remaining soy sauce, sugar and sesame oil. Return the beef and mushrooms to the wok and toss to heat through.

+ Transfer the beef mixture to a serving plate. Quickly toss the cooked noodles in the wok with any remaining sauce to heat through, then place on the serving plate beside the beef. Sprinkle with the sesame seeds and pine nuts and serve immediately.

NOTES

You can use mung bean noodles or other dried noodles instead of soba. But I love the taste of soba noodles with this marinade.

Stir-fry some gochujang (Korean hot bean paste) (see Note page 22) in with the beef to give it a deep rich flavour. If you don't have that on hand, add a teaspoon of chilli flakes, it will really get the party started.

Blue swimmer crab tagliatelle with lemon and chilli

The crab in this recipe is already cooked then just warmed through by the heat of the pasta. You can also sauté raw blue swimmer crabmeat before adding it to the tagliatelle. Its texture is different from that of the usual boiled and picked crabmeat.

SERVES 4

+ Segment 6 of the lemons. To do this, cut off both ends of each lemon so you can see the flesh and sit them flat on a chopping board. Working from top to bottom, cut off the skin and pith. Cut just inside a segment membrane to the middle of the lemon, repeat on the other side and the segment should fall out. Have a large bowl ready to catch the segments and any juice that is left.

+ Shred the rocket leaves, then place in the bowl with the lemon segments. Add the crabmeat, chilli, anchovies, olive oil and the juice of the remaining 4 lemons. Season to taste with sea salt and white pepper and stir gently.

+ Cook the tagliatelle in a saucepan of well-salted boiling water for about 8 minutes or until *al dente*. Drain, but leave a little cooking water still clinging to the pasta to keep it moist.

+ Quickly add the pasta to the bowl with the lemon and rocket mixture and toss well. Divide among four large pasta bowls. Sprinkle with breadcrumbs, if you like, parmesan, and a generous grind of white pepper. Serve immediately.

600 g (1 lb 5 oz) cooked blue
    swimmer crabmeat
10 lemons
4 bunches rocket (arugula)
    (about 500 g/1 lb 2 oz), washed
    and trimmed
8 long fresh red chillies, seeded
    and finely chopped
6 anchovy fillets, finely chopped
200 ml (7 fl oz) extra virgin olive oil
sea salt and freshly ground
    white pepper
800 g (1 lb 12 oz) good-quality
    dried tagliatelle
toasted coarse breadcrumbs
    (optional) and freshly grated
    parmesan, to serve

NOTE

Freshly toasted breadcrumbs add a wonderful texture, you can embellish them by toasting them on a baking sheet with crushed garlic and then folding in a bit of chopped parsley. I also don't mind grated cheese on this, most Italians would be ready to kill me, but you do see seafood and cheese in Sicilian cooking.

Buffalo mozzarella lasagne

This is an awesome lasagne. Don't be daunted by the long list of ingredients — they're all readily available, and the dish is so easy to put together.

SERVES 6

+ Preheat the oven to 190°C (375°F/Gas 5). Adjust the oven racks so the dish can sit in the middle.

+ To make the meat sauce, heat the olive oil in a large heavy-based frying pan over medium heat. Cook the onion, stirring occasionally, until softened but not browned. Add the garlic and cook until fragrant. Increase the heat to medium–high and add the meats and a pinch of sea salt and white pepper. Cook, breaking up the meat with a wooden spoon, for 4 minutes or until it loses its raw colour but is not browned. Add the flour and cook, stirring, for 2 minutes. Add the vinegar and cook, stirring occasionally, until it has almost evaporated. Add the sugar, passata and tomatoes and simmer for 10 minutes or until the sauce thickens slightly. Check the seasoning, stir in the basil and set the meat sauce aside.

+ To make the béchamel, melt the butter in a heavy-based saucepan over low–medium heat. Add the flour and cook, stirring, for 1–2 minutes. Remove the pan from the heat and, whisking continuously to avoid any lumps forming, add the milk all at once. Return the pan to the heat and keep whisking, until the sauce boils and thickens to the consistency of thickened cream. Remove from the heat and season to taste.

+ To assemble the lasagne, spread a quarter of the meat sauce in the base of a 2.5 litre (87 fl oz/10 cup) capacity dish. Cover the meat sauce with a layer of lasagne sheets to fit. Spread another quarter of the sauce over the pasta, then a third of the torn mozzarella. Continue layering the pasta, meat sauce and mozzarella two more times. Pour the béchamel sauce evenly over the final layer of mozzarella, then sprinkle with the parmesan. Bake on the middle shelf of the oven for 30 minutes or until the cheese is brown and the sauce is bubbling. Let the lasagne stand for 10 minutes before serving.

9 instant lasagne sheets
500 g (1 lb 2 oz) fresh buffalo or
   cow's milk mozzarella, torn
   into pieces
100 g (3½ oz/¾ cup) freshly grated
   parmesan

Meat sauce

1 tablespoon extra virgin olive oil
1 onion, finely chopped
6 garlic cloves, finely chopped
300 g (10½ oz) minced (ground) pork
300 g (10½ oz) minced (ground) veal
sea salt and freshly ground
   white pepper
2 teaspoons plain (all-purpose) flour
2 tablespoons balsamic vinegar
pinch of caster (superfine) sugar
700 ml (24 fl oz) tomato passata
   (puréed tomatoes)
400 g (14 oz) tin diced tomatoes
2 large handfuls basil leaves

Béchamel sauce

50 g (1¾ oz) unsalted butter
2 tablespoons plain (all-purpose) flour
600 ml (21 fl oz) milk

NOTES

The meat sauce can be cooled, covered and refrigerated for up to 2 days. Just reheat it before you assemble the lasagne.

For perfect entertaining, you can prepare and cook the lasagne well ahead of time. Then, when friends arrive for dinner, all you have to do is heat it up, prepare a salad and open the wine.

Chargrilled baby octopus with olives and hand-pounded pesto

Whether it's over wood, charcoal or gas, chargrilling gives a lovely, smoky flavour to your favourite seafood or steak.

SERVES 4

+ Pound the garlic and ½ teaspoon of sea salt to a paste in a mortar and pestle. Add the basil and continue to pound until the basil breaks down and a thick paste has formed. Add the pine nuts and work them in well so the paste has a creamy texture.

+ Add the parmesan, olive oil and lemon juice, season to taste with white pepper and combine well. Transfer the pesto to a large bowl and stir in the olives and cherry tomatoes.

+ Cook the octopus in a chargrill pan over high heat for 5 minutes or until it gets good colour and char marks. You want that nice barbecue flavour. Cut the octopus into bite-sized pieces or leave whole if you prefer, then add to the pesto mix and toss to combine well.

+ To serve, place a small pile of salad leaves on each of four serving plates. Top with the octopus and pesto mixture, drizzle with extra virgin olive oil and serve immediately.

500 g (1 lb 2 oz) baby octopus, cleaned
80 g (2¾ oz/⅓ cup) Ligurian olives, pitted
12 cherry tomatoes, quartered
100 g (3½ oz) mixed salad leaves, washed

Pesto

½ small garlic clove
sea salt and freshly ground white pepper
½ bunch basil, leaves picked
20 g (¾ oz) pine nuts
1 tablespoon finely grated parmesan
2 tablespoons extra virgin olive oil, plus extra, for drizzling
1 tablespoon lemon juice

NOTES

Make the effort to hand-pound the pesto — you will never again use a blender. The pesto is great with pasta or other salads.

Don't toast the pine nuts; they will overpower the pesto.

The octopus can be replaced with other seafood, and roast chicken also makes a handy substitute.

Roast blue-eye trevalla with fennel and olives

This dish is wonderfully rustic, and the combination of fennel, tomato, olives and chilli is unsurpassed for fish. Large pieces of any white-fleshed fish will suit this dish.

SERVES 4

+ Preheat the oven to 200°C (400°F/Gas 6).

+ Scatter the fennel, onion, oregano and thyme in the base of a baking dish (make sure it will fit 4 fish fillets fairly snugly). Drizzle the vegetables and herbs with most of the olive oil. Mix through the capsicum, tomato, capers, anchovies, olives and chilli flakes. Season liberally with sea salt and white pepper and pour over the wine. Roast for 1 hour or until the vegetables are tender and the tomatoes are melting to form a sauce.

+ Remove the dish from the oven, snuggle the fish down into the sauce, drizzle with the remaining oil and sprinkle with sea salt. Roast for about 10 minutes more, or until the fish is just cooked through.

+ To serve, place a fillet on each of four plates, spoon over the sauce, then sprinkle with parsley and serve with a wedge of lemon. Serve with a green salad, if desired.

NOTE

This fish dish is also easy to do on top of the stove. Just sweat the vegetables slowly in olive oil, add a cup of wine and cover. Cook for 1 hour over a low heat at a very gentle simmer, then add the fish and cook, uncovered, for about 10 minutes. Turn the fish halfway through cooking.

4 blue-eye trevalla fillets, about 200 g (7 oz) each, skin off
1 fennel bulb, trimmed and thinly sliced
1 red onion, thinly sliced
2 tablespoons oregano leaves, chopped
2 tablespoons thyme leaves, chopped
60 ml (2 fl oz/¼ cup) extra virgin olive oil
1 red capsicum (pepper), halved, seeded and thinly sliced
4 vine-ripened tomatoes, peeled, seeded and quartered
2 tablespoons salted baby capers, rinsed and drained
6 anchovy fillets
150 g (5½ oz) Ligurian olives
1 teaspoon chilli flakes
sea salt and freshly ground white pepper
250 ml (9 fl oz/1 cup) white wine
2 tablespoons chopped flat-leaf (Italian) parsley leaves
lemon wedges, to serve
green salad, to serve (optional)

Whole salt-baked ocean trout

The salt crust surrounding the trout keeps the fish moist. Serve it just above room temperature and with any sauce you like; salsa verde or chimichurri would be delicious.

SERVES 6–8

+ Preheat the oven to 220°C (425°F/Gas 7).

+ Sprinkle the cavity of the fish with sea salt. Coarsely tear the dill and place it in the cavity, along with the lemon wedges.

+ Spread a large baking tray with a 1 cm (½ inch) layer of table salt. Place the fish on top of the salt and cover it with the remaining salt. Sprinkle 60 ml (2 fl oz/¼ cup) water over the salt; this will help to form the crust.

+ Bake the fish for 25 minutes, then remove from the oven and rest for 10 minutes.

+ Break the crust from the top of the fish (most likely, the skin will come off with it). Remove any remaining skin and discard. To fillet the fish, cut in a line down the spine and remove the flesh in large chunks. Break the spine at the head and tail and remove. Take the fillets from the second side.

+ Divide the fish among the serving plates, drizzle with extra virgin olive oil, a squeeze of lemon and finish with a generous grind of white pepper. Serve with a dollop of aïoli on the side.

Aïoli

MAKES ABOUT 400 ML (14 FL OZ)

+ Put a saucepan large enough to hold a stainless-steel bowl on a work surface. Place a tea towel (dish towel) around the inside edge of the pan and place the bowl on top; this will hold the bowl steady while you whisk.

+ Put the egg yolks in the bowl and whisk. Add the garlic, lemon juice and sea salt to taste and, while whisking, drizzle in the olive oil very slowly. As the emulsion starts to form, add the oil in a steady stream. Don't let the oil sit on the surface as this can cause the aïoli to split. Add a grind of white pepper and check the seasoning for salt and lemon juice.

+ Serve immediately or keep in the refrigerator for up to 1 week.

1.8 kg (4 lb) whole ocean trout
sea salt and freshly ground
  white pepper
1 bunch dill
2 lemons, 1 cut into 6 wedges,
  the other halved
5 kg (11 lb 4 oz) table salt
extra virgin olive oil, for drizzling
aïoli, to serve (see recipe below)

Aïoli

3 free-range egg yolks
3–4 garlic cloves, crushed
2 tablespoons lemon juice
sea salt
375 ml (13 fl oz/1½ cups) half
  olive oil, half extra virgin olive oil
sea salt and freshly ground
  white pepper

NOTE

Bake the fish until a thermometer registers an internal temperature of 56°C (133°F) and always rest the fish for 10 minutes to allow the heat to set the flesh.

Crumbed leatherjacket with steamed zucchini

Crisp crumbed fish and simply prepared zucchini are a great match. Leatherjacket has a mild flavour and nice flaky texture. It is a great fish to serve whole to kids as there are no small bones.

SERVES 4

+ Place the zucchini in a steamer and cook over boiling water for about 12 minutes or until very soft. Transfer the zucchini to a bowl and drizzle with the olive oil. Add the lemon juice and parsley and season with sea salt and white pepper. Mix with a fork to lightly mash the zucchini. Set aside.

+ Set up a crumbing station with three bowls containing (from left to right) flour, egg wash and breadcrumbs. Add a clean plate for your crumbed fish. Coat a fish fillet in flour and shake off the excess, then dip it in egg wash, then in the breadcrumbs to coat all over. Shake off the excess and set aside. Repeat with the remaining fish.

+ Place the vegetable oil in a saucepan large enough to take 3–4 fish fillets at a time or a deep-fryer, and heat the oil to 180°C (350°F) or until a cube of bread dropped into the oil turns golden brown in 15 seconds. (It must stay at that temperature during the entire process, so don't overcrowd the fryer during cooking.) Line an oven tray with paper towel. Deep-fry the fish fillets, in batches for 2–3 minutes or until golden. Place on the prepared tray and keep warm. Repeat with the remaining fish.

+ Meanwhile, reheat the zucchini gently in a saucepan and divide among four plates.

+ Place 2 fish fillets and a lemon wedge on each plate, sprinkle with sea salt and give a good grind of white pepper. Serve immediately.

700 g (1 lb 9 oz) leatherjacket fillets (about 80 g/2¾ oz each)
400 g (14 oz) zucchini (courgettes), trimmed and cut into 1 cm (½ inch) discs
60 ml (¼ cup) extra virgin olive oil
juice of 1 lemon
8 or so flat-leaf (Italian) parsley leaves, chopped
sea salt and freshly ground white pepper
150 g (5½ oz/1 cup) plain (all-purpose) flour, lightly seasoned
1 free-range egg, beaten with 1 cup (9 fl oz/250 ml) milk, for egg wash
110 g (3¾ oz/1 cup) fine dried breadcrumbs
vegetable oil, for deep-frying
lemon wedges, to serve

NOTES

The steamed zucchini makes a wonderful, simple sauce for fresh pasta.

To make a similar mash, you can also peel, slice and steam small eggplants (aubergines) until tender. This rocks with just about any protein. And a good whack of chopped fresh chilli will really get it going.

King prawns with spaghetti and cherry tomato vinaigrette

Simple vinaigrettes are terrific with pasta. Plus, when tomatoes are in season they are simply perfect with seafood.

SERVES 4

+ Cook the pasta in a large saucepan of well-salted boiling water for about 8 minutes or until *al dente*, then drain.

+ Meanwhile, heat the olive oil in a large frying pan over medium heat. Add the chilli and sauté for 30 seconds. Remove the pan from the heat and add the prawns, tomatoes, vinegar and sea salt and white pepper to taste and combine. Add the basil and parsley and, finally, the drained pasta and toss to combine well. Transfer to a serving bowl and scatter with the toasted breadcrumbs and extra herbs.

16 cooked king prawn (shrimp), peeled, deveined and roughly chopped
400 g (14 oz) spaghetti
150 ml (5 fl oz) extra virgin olive oil
3–4 small fresh red chillies, seeded and finely chopped
250 g (9 oz) sweet cherry tomatoes, quartered
60 ml (2 fl oz/¼ cup) good-quality red wine vinegar
sea salt and freshly ground white pepper
2 tablespoons roughly chopped basil, plus extra, to serve
2 tablespoons roughly chopped flat-leaf (Italian) parsley, plus extra, to serve
toasted coarse breadcrumbs, to serve

NOTES

Leave the prawns whole if you like, but I think this dish is easier to eat and has a more complete flavour with little pieces of prawn mixed through.

Freshly toasted breadcrumbs add a wonderful texture.

I often finely chop ripe tomatoes, add sea salt, pepper, chilli and extra virgin olive oil, and toss through hot spaghetti for a satisfying lunch. Add lashings of freshly grated parmesan, too.

Roast duck legs with apricots

Apricots are a great garnish with roast duck, chicken or pork. Peaches this way are terrific, too, just add a little more water so the peaches can cook. If the fruit gets very soft then remove it when you are reducing the water down to a dressing with the spices and onions.

SERVES 4

+ Preheat the oven to 200°C (400°F/Gas 6).

+ Prick the skin on the duck legs with a fork, then sprinkle all over with sea salt and rub with 2 tablespoons of the extra virgin olive oil. Put the duck legs on a wire rack in a roasting pan and roast for 15 minutes. Reduce the oven temperature to 160°C (315°F/Gas 2–3) and cook for another 30–40 minutes or until the duck is cooked. Remove from the oven, cover with foil and rest for 10 minutes.

+ Meanwhile, heat the butter and remaining oil in a saucepan large enough to hold the apricots in a single layer over medium heat. Add the onion and ginger and cook, stirring regularly, for 10 minutes or until soft. Add the spices, honey and sea salt to taste and cook for another minute. Add the apricots, cut side down, drizzle over the balsamic vinegar, then add 250 ml (9 fl oz/1 cup) water and cover with a lid or foil. After about 10 minutes remove the lid and simmer the water away, the apricots should be tender, but don't let them fall apart. Squeeze the lemon juice in, check for salt and give a good grind of white pepper.

+ Place 2 duck legs on each of the four plates, place two apricot halves next to the duck and spoon the pan juices over the duck.

8 duck Marylands or 2 whole ducks if you prefer
sea salt and freshly ground white pepper
125 ml (4 fl oz/½ cup) extra virgin olive oil
40 g (1½ oz) butter
1 small red onion, finely diced
2 tablespoons finely chopped ginger
1 teaspoon ground cinnamon
1 teaspoon ground ginger
60 g (2¼ oz) honey
4 fresh apricots, halved and seeded
80 ml (2½ fl oz/⅓ cup) balsamic vinegar
juice of 1 lemon

Braised chicken and rice, Korean style

I love the Korean flavours in this one-bowl dish with rice. Rice might just be the ultimate comfort food. Take inspiration from Korea.

SERVES 4

+ To make the seasoning, combine all the ingredients in a bowl and set aside for 10 minutes to let the flavours blend.

+ Place the chicken in a large saucepan with the vegetables and eggs (still in the shell) and just cover with water. Bring to the boil, skimming any froth from the surface. Pour in the seasoning mixture and simmer gently for 20 minutes or until everything is tender.

+ To serve, divide the rice among four bowls. With a slotted spoon, divide the chicken and vegetables among the bowls. Remove the eggs, then return the broth to the stove and bring to the boil.

+ Meanwhile, peel the eggs and cut in half. Add half a boiled egg to each bowl, pour over some of the reduced sauce and serve.

NOTES

Use any vegetables you like. The same goes for the meat; use your favourite protein. You'll just have to adjust the cooking time.

Instead of boiling the eggs, you can whisk them and cook a thin omelette. Roll it up and cut it into thin strips and add to the dish for amazing texture and flavour.

8 free-range chicken thighs (organic if possible), bone in, skin on and chopped in half
1 large waxy potato (such as bintje or nicola varieties), peeled and cut into 2.5 cm (1 inch) cubes
1 large carrot, peeled and cut into 2.5 cm (1 inch) cubes
3 brown onions, each cut into 6 wedges
2 large free-range eggs
210 g (7½ oz/1 cup) short-grain sushi rice, cooked and kept warm
1 teaspoon sesame seeds, toasted, to serve (optional)
2 spring onions (scallions), cut into rounds with some of the dark-green part, to serve (optional)

Seasoning

185 ml (6 fl oz/¾ cup) light soy sauce
55 g (2 oz/¼ cup) sugar
30 g (1 oz/¼ cup) finely chopped spring onions (scallions)
4 garlic cloves, crushed
2 tablespoons finely chopped ginger
60 ml (2 fl oz/¼ cup) Shaoxing rice wine
pinch of freshly ground black pepper
1 teaspoon sesame oil

Buttermilk fried chook

Who doesn't like crispy chicken? There are always several recipes for it in every culture. Some of my favourite Asian dishes have fried chicken as their centrepiece.

SERVES 4

+ Fill a deep-fryer or saucepan two-thirds full of oil and heat to 180°C (350°F). If you are using a saucepan then use a kitchen thermometer as a guide as you don't want the oil too hot.

+ Combine all the coating ingredients in a large bowl, then split it between two medium bowls. Pour the buttermilk into a third bowl and season to taste. Now place the bowls in a line starting with one bowl of coating, followed by the milk, then the other bowl of coating, and a tray or plate at the end for the coated chicken.

+ Dip each chicken thigh into the first bowl of coating, patting off any excess and then dip into the buttermilk, allowing the excess milk to run off back into the bowl; then dip into the second bowl of coating. Place on the plate or tray and repeat until all the chicken thighs are coated.

+ Working in batches, gradually lower the thighs into the hot oil. If using a saucepan of oil rather than a deep-fryer, make sure you adjust the temperature to get it back to 180°C (350°F) as quickly as possible. Fry for 2–3 minutes, then carefully move the chicken pieces around in the oil and continue to fry, for a further 12–14 minutes. The chicken should be golden brown and very crisp. Drain on paper towel and serve with lemon wedges, potato salad and coleslaw.

8 free-range chicken thighs (organic if possible), bone in, skin on
vegetable oil, for deep-frying
600 ml (21 fl oz) buttermilk
lemon wedges, potato salad and coleslaw, to serve (see Note)

Coating

600 g (1 lb 5 oz/4 cups) plain (all-purpose) flour
2 tablespoons garlic powder
3 tablespoons onion powder
1 teaspoon paprika
½ teaspoon chilli powder
1 teaspoon sea salt
freshly ground white pepper, to taste

NOTES

I like to cook wings in the same coating and you can toss them with herbs and a Thai nam jin dressing or Vietnamese nuoc cham for a delightful salad with rice. They are also great tossed in a little melted butter laced with lashings of Tabasco for a hot wings and beer fix.

To make an easy potato salad, simply boil whole small or halved pink eye potatoes until tender. Drain, then crush lightly, season with sea salt and pepper, drizzle with extra virgin olive oil (the potatoes will drink quite a bit) and sprinkle with either red wine vinegar or lemon juice. Thinly sliced parsley makes a welcome flavour and colour addition.

For a coleslaw, just shave cabbage finely, add grated carrot and onion and mix with mayonnaise or aïoli (see page 102).

Hamburger with thrice-cooked chips

Hamburgers are all about the meat. I season the mince with salt only, and I'm not even a big believer in salad on them.

SERVES 4

+ Place the meat in a bowl and sprinkle with about ½–¾ teaspoon salt. Mix gently, then divide into four portions. Move each portion from hand to hand for 2 minutes to make a firm but not overworked patty, then shape into a ball. Gently flatten to form 2 cm (¾ inch) patties. (If you're making the patties the day before, cover and store in the refrigerator, but take them out of the refrigerator well before cooking so they are close to room temperature when you do cook them. This will ensure even cooking and help the patties retain the heat from the barbecue or pan.)

+ Heat a barbecue or a frying pan to very hot. Brush extra virgin olive oil over the patties and cook for 6 minutes, then turn and cook for another 6 minutes (for medium-rare) or until done to your liking. Set the patties aside to rest for 5 minutes. If you want a plain burger, just place a patty on a bun, add sauce and serve.

+ For a more elaborate burger, place a slice of cheese on each patty to soften as it rests, and cook the bacon on the barbecue. Toast the buns on both cut sides.

+ Place the bun bases on four plates. On each bun, place lettuce, a patty with cheese, bacon, sauce, tomato and, if you wish, pickled cucumber. Add a grind of white pepper. Top each with a bun lid and serve with hot chips (see Chips recipe, page 114).

1 kg (2 lb 4 oz) freshly ground
   chuck steak
sea salt and freshly ground
   white pepper
extra virgin olive oil, for brushing
4 hamburger buns, split
4 slices Gruyère
4 rashers good-quality smoked bacon
lettuce leaves and tomato slices
tomato sauce (ketchup), barbecue
   sauce or mustard (any combination
   you like)
sliced pickled cucumber (optional)

HOT TIPS

Personally, I like my burgers cooked on the medium-rare or medium side as I think it's important for them to be juicy, but, by all means, cook them to your liking.

Ask your butcher to mince the beef freshly for you. Then it will be extra fresh and make all the difference to the dish.

If you barbecue your patties and bacon outside over charcoal or wood, your reward will be tenfold. I love a smoky taste on my burgers.

Chips

Thanks to British chef Heston Blumenthal, we all need to thrice-cook our chips now. But it really is worth the effort — the steaming and double-frying renders a crisp chip that is creamy on the inside and stays crunchy longer. This is my version.

SERVES 4 AS A SIDE DISH

+ Peel and cut the potatoes into 1 cm (½ inch) slices, then chips about 1 cm (½ inch) wide. Wash them well in cold water to remove some of the starch.

+ Lay the chips in a steamer and steam for 15–20 minutes or until half cooked. Spread out on a paper towel-lined tray and stand until slightly cooled, then refrigerate until cold.

+ Make sure you remove all of the moisture, by wrapping in a clean towel (dish towel), or the chips will spit.

+ Using a thermometer as a guide, heat the oil in a large saucepan or a deep-fryer to about 170°C (325°F). Deep-fry the chips in batches for 5 minutes without browning, then drain on paper towel, cool and refrigerate until ready to serve.

+ When ready to serve, heat the oil to 180°C (350°F) and cook the chips in batches for about 3 minutes until they are golden brown. Drain again on paper towels. Sprinkle the chips liberally with sea salt and serve immediately.

300 g (10½ oz) waxy potatoes
  (such as bintje)
vegetable oil, for deep-frying
sea salt

Spicy lamb and sweet potato curry

Don't be put off by the long list of ingredients. This is a simple boiled curry; it truly doesn't come any easier!

SERVES 4

+ For the spice paste, pound all the ingredients in a mortar with a pestle, or use a blender, to make a fine paste, adding a little water if necessary.

+ For the curry, heat a wok over high heat until just smoking. Add the oil and, when hot, add the spice paste and stir-fry for about 5 minutes, or until the rawness has gone and the paste is fragrant.

+ Add 1 litre (35 fl oz/4 cups) water and bring to the boil. Add the lamb, lime leaves and lemongrass, then reduce the heat to low, cover and simmer gently for 45 minutes. Remove the lid and simmer for a further 15 minutes, or until the lamb is tender and the sauce has reduced and thickened slightly.

+ Meanwhile, steam the sweet potato for 15–20 minutes, or until tender. Stir it into the curry, then season with the palm sugar, fish sauce and lime juice. Serve with steamed rice and greens — snow peas (mangetout) would be nice.

500 g (1 lb 2 oz) trimmed lamb shoulder, cut into 2 cm (¾ inch) dice
80 ml (2½ fl oz/⅓ cup) vegetable oil
5 kaffir lime leaves
2 lemongrass stems, outer leaves removed, bruised and cut into 4 cm (1½ inch) lengths
300 g (10½ oz) sweet potato, peeled and cut into 2 cm (¾ inch) dice
1½ tablespoons grated palm sugar (jaggery)
1½ teaspoons fish sauce
juice of 1 lime
steamed rice and greens, to serve

Spice paste

2 teaspoons black peppercorns
8 candlenuts (available from Asian grocers), roasted until golden, chopped
4 long green chillies, seeded and chopped
2 long fresh red chillies, seeded and chopped
4 small wild green chillies (available from Asian grocers), chopped
4 red Asian shallots, chopped
3 cm (1¼ inch) knob of galangal, chopped
2 cm (¾ inch) knob of ginger, peeled and chopped
2 fingers fresh turmeric, chopped
1 teaspoon sea salt

Barbecued lamb leg with cumin, lemongrass and ginger

Butterflying is a terrific way to deal with a leg of lamb. Have your butcher prepare it and away you go: you should have a nice rectangle of meat to fit easily on the barbie. Lamb absolutely loves cumin. I like to use a combination of ground and whole, lightly crushed seeds, because it adds a pleasing texture. If you want an easier option, lamb cutlets are good, and chicken loves this marinade as well.

SERVES 8

+ To make the marinade, put the garlic, lemongrass, ginger, cumin and salt in a mortar and pound into a rough paste with a pestle. Add the herbs and pound for a further minute, then stir in the olive oil and mix well. You can also process in a food processor or blender if you wish, but don't make too smooth a paste. Spread the marinade evenly over the lamb and leave for at least an hour out of the refrigerator before cooking.

+ Preheat the barbecue and make sure the grill bars are clean. (If you don't have a barbecue, heat a heavy-based frying pan to very hot.) When hot, put the lamb on the hottest part. Cook for about 6 minutes on each side for medium-rare. Put on a platter and cover with foil. Rest in a warm place for 10 minutes.

+ Carve the lamb into 5 mm (¼ inch) slices and arrange on a platter. Mix a little extra oil with the juices on the resting platter and pour over the lamb. Give a good grind of black pepper and serve immediately with Italian-style coleslaw, vine-ripened tomato salad and lemon wedges, if desired.

1 boneless lamb leg (about 2 kg/ 4 lb 8 oz), butterflied
freshly ground black pepper and lemon wedges, to serve (optional)
Italian-style coleslaw and vine-ripened tomato salad, to serve (see Notes)

Marinade

2 garlic cloves, chopped
2 lemongrass stems, outer leaves removed, thinly sliced
3 cm (1¼ inch) knob of ginger, chopped
2 teaspoons toasted cumin seeds, half crushed to a powder, the rest left whole
1 teaspoon sea salt
¼ cup chopped coriander (cilantro) leaves
¼ cup chopped mint
60 ml (2 fl oz/¼ cup) extra virgin olive oil, plus extra, to serve

NOTES

To make an Italian-style coleslaw, firstly finely shred 1 baby cabbage or half a Savoy cabbage. Put the cabbage a large bowl and season with sea salt and freshly ground black pepper. Drizzle with extra virgin olive oil and red wine vinegar, at a ratio of three parts oil to one part vinegar. Start to toss the cabbage. Don't add so much dressing that it becomes wet, just enough to moisten. Toss through freshly shaved parmesan as you like; I like a lot. Serve as a shared starter or a salad with the main.

To make a simple vine-ripened tomato salad, cut 8 small vine-ripened tomatoes into chunks. Sprinkle with sea salt. Give a good grind of fresh black pepper and drizzle with extra virgin olive oil and balsamic vinegar.

Tagine of lamb with couscous and an orange, almond and chopped date salad

One of my favourite tagines is the classic lamb, here paired with the sweetness of sweet potato. The vegetables can be added to or swapped to reflect your likes and dislikes.

SERVES 4

+ For the chermoula, purée all the ingredients, except the olive oil, in a food processor. With the motor running, add the oil slowly to make a wet paste.

+ Place the lamb in a dish, add half the chermoula paste and rub all over the lamb. Stand for 1 hour.

+ Heat the olive oil in a frying pan with a tight-fitting lid over high heat. When hot, fry the lamb for 5 minutes (this may need to be done in batches) until it is well coloured. Add the pumpkin, the remaining chermoula paste, lemon juice, honey, sea salt to taste and 750 ml (26 fl oz/3 cups) water. Bring to the boil, then reduce the heat to low, cover and simmer gently for 1½ hours or until the meat is tender. Fold in the chickpeas to warm them.

+ To prepare the couscous, place the butter, olive oil and 400 ml (14 fl oz) boiling water in a bowl with a pinch of salt. Cover with foil and stand for 2 minutes or until the butter has melted. While stirring, add the couscous, and when the liquid is absorbed, fluff with a fork.

+ Transfer the couscous to a basket steamer lined with a tea towel (dish towel) or muslin (cheesecloth). Set over a saucepan of boiling water and steam for 20 minutes, or until tender.

+ For the orange salad, juice 1 of the oranges, then peel and segment the remaining oranges. Combine all the ingredients and refrigerate until chilled.

+ To serve, place some couscous into each of four bowls, spoon the tagine on top and serve with the orange, almond and chopped date salad on the side.

> *NOTES*
>
> *Add dried fruits such as dates, apricots or raisins to give the tagine an extra sweet-and-sour taste.*
>
> *Pomegranate seeds are a sensational addition to this salad for that extra dimension of crunch, colour and flavour.*

700 g (1 lb 9 oz) trimmed lamb shoulder, cut into 3 cm (1¼ inch) dice
60 ml (2 fl oz/¼ cup) extra virgin olive oil
500 g (1 lb 2 oz) butternut pumpkin, (squash) peeled and cut into 3 cm (1¼ inch) dice
juice of 1 lemon
2 tablespoons honey
sea salt
200 g (7 oz) tinned chickpeas, drained and rinsed

Chermoula

juice of 1 lemon
½ bunch flat-leaf (Italian) parsley, leaves picked
1 bunch coriander (cilantro), well washed
1 red onion, thinly sliced into half moons
4 garlic cloves
2 tablespoons *ras el hanout* (North African spice mix)
1 tablespoon sea salt
1 teaspoon ground ginger
1 teaspoon ground cumin
1 teaspoon mild chilli powder
½ teaspoon ground turmeric
125 ml (4 fl oz/½ cup) olive oil

Couscous

100 g (3½ oz) butter
2 tablespoons extra virgin olive oil
400 g (14 oz) couscous

Orange, almond and chopped date salad

4 oranges
2 tablespoons caster (superfine) sugar
2 tablespoons extra virgin olive oil
pinch of sea salt
ground cinnamon, to taste
100 g (3½ oz) chopped dates
100 g (3½ oz) slivered almonds

Barbecued pork chops with apple, potato, parsley and lemon salad

The golden rule for perfect barbecued pork chops? Don't overcook them.

SERVES 4

+ Remove the chops from the refrigerator 2 hours before you intend to start cooking, and season liberally with sea salt.

+ Using a microplane, grate half the zest of 1 lemon into a bowl. Cut the top and bottom off the lemon and, with a paring knife, remove the remaining skin and pith and discard. Segment the lemon and add the segments to the bowl with the zest. Squeeze the juice from the second lemon into the bowl.

+ Melt the butter in a small non-stick frying pan over medium heat. Add the apples and cook for about 5 minutes or until soft. Remove from the heat and when cool, place in the bowl with the lemon.

+ Meanwhile, place the potatoes in a saucepan and cover with cold water. Bring to the boil and cook for about 5 minutes or until tender. Drain and, when cool, add to the lemon and apple mixture. Add the parsley and oil, season to taste and toss gently.

+ Preheat the barbecue to hot. Splash the chops with a little olive oil and shake off any excess. For nice crisscross grill marks, place the chops on the grill bars and cook for 2–3 minutes. Rotate the chops 90 degrees and cook for a further 2–3 minutes. Turn them over and cook for 5 minutes or until done to your liking. Place the chops on a plate, cover with foil to keep warm and allow them to rest for 10 minutes.

+ Place a chop on each of four plates, drizzle with any resting juices, sprinkle with sea salt and white pepper and serve with the salad.

4 free-range pork chops, about
   250–300 g (9–10½ oz) each
sea salt and freshly ground
   white pepper
2 lemons
80 g (2¾ oz) unsalted butter
2 granny smith apples, peeled,
   cored and cut into 8 pieces
2 large kipfler potatoes, peeled
   and cut into 8 pieces
1 handful flat-leaf (Italian)
   parsley leaves
60 ml (2 fl oz/¼ cup) extra virgin
   olive oil, plus extra, for cooking

NOTES

The pork is great drizzled with aged balsamic vinegar.

Try the salad with dried fruit such as dates, prunes or apricots. I also like it with a chopped jalapeño chilli or two folded through. Or you can replace the lemon juice with 1–2 tablespoons verjuice.

Stir-fried pork with snake beans and black fungi

**This is perfect as part of an Asian-inspired banquet lunch —
a little bit Thai, a little bit Chinese. Just add steamed rice
and boiled greens and it's deliciously balanced.**

SERVES 4 AS PART OF A SHARED BANQUET

+ Place the pork belly in a saucepan of cold water and bring to the boil. Drain and rinse the pork (this gets rid of any scum). Place the pork in a saucepan of salted water and bring to the boil. Simmer gently for 1½ hours or until the pork is tender. Drain and pat dry with paper towel.

+ Heat a wok over high heat until smoking. Add 2 tablespoons of the peanut oil and, when hot, stir-fry the pork in two batches until golden and crisp. Be very careful at this point as any liquid in the pork can make the hot oil spit. Set the cooked pork aside and wipe the wok clean.

+ Heat the remaining oil in the wok until just smoking. Stir-fry the ginger, garlic, spring onion and chilli until fragrant. Add the beans and snow peas and stir-fry until just tender. Add the pork, chicken stock, oyster and soy sauces and sugar, toss together and bring to the boil. Fold in the black fungi then serve immediately.

400 g (14 oz) boneless pork belly, cut into 3 cm (1¼ inch) squares
80 ml (2½ fl oz/⅓ cup) peanut oil
2 cm (¾ inch) knob of ginger, peeled and finely chopped
2 garlic cloves, finely chopped
2 spring onions (scallions), finely chopped
1 long fresh red chilli, seeded and finely chopped
6 snake (yard-long) beans, cut into 4 cm (1½ inch) lengths
10 snow peas (mangetout), trimmed
60 ml (2 fl oz/¼ cup) chicken stock
2 tablespoons oyster sauce
2 teaspoons light soy sauce
1 teaspoon sugar
80 g (2¾ oz) fresh black fungi (available from Asian grocers), cut into julienne

NOTES

To simplify this dish, you could use pork fillet or leg and omit the first cooking. However, belly, even though it takes double cooking, is worth the effort.

Go the extra yard! If you are a chilli fiend like me, a few fresh chillies cut into rounds and added to the pork are a welcome addition.

Chocolate and cognac cake

This cake is so moreish. It's an elegant, indulgent way to finish a great meal. All this cake needs is a dollop of whipped cream.

SERVES 10–12

+ Preheat the oven to 170°C (325°F/Gas 3). Cut a piece of baking paper to fit a 20 cm (8 inch) round cake tin, with a double layer for the side and a single layer for the base. Spray the tin with cooking oil and fit the baking paper snugly. Don't use a springform tin here — it needs to be solid.

+ Melt the chocolate in a stainless-steel bowl set over a saucepan of hot water ensuring the base of the bowl doesn't touch the water. Don't let the water boil, as you can scald the chocolate. Remove the chocolate from the heat and let it return to room temperature.

+ Using an electric mixer, beat the egg yolks and 100 g (3½ oz) of the caster sugar until pale and creamy. Add the cognac and continue to beat until well combined. Add the chocolate and stir until completely incorporated, then slowly stir in half the cream. Set aside.

+ Whip the remaining cream until soft peaks form. Set aside. Whisk the egg whites in a very clean bowl until soft peaks form, then slowly add the remaining caster sugar and whisk until very firm. Fold the whipped cream into the chocolate mixture, then gently fold in the egg whites.

+ Pour the cake mixture into the prepared tin, place the tin in a deep roasting tin and add enough hot water to come 2.5 cm (1 inch) up the side of the tin. Bake for 45 minutes, then turn the oven temperature down to 150°C (300°F/Gas 2) and bake for another 45 minutes. Turn the oven off and leave the cake in the oven for 40 minutes, then remove to a wire rack. Run a knife around the inside edge of the tin and turn it onto a plate or a board — the cake should slide out easily but be extremely careful as the cake is so soft and fragile. Sprinkle with cocoa powder or icing sugar. To slice the cake, use a knife dipped in hot water and clean the knife after each cut. You will only want a slither per person as this cake is so rich.

400 g (14 oz) good-quality dark chocolate (I use Valrhona 53% cocoa solids), broken up
6 free-range eggs, separated
150 g (5½ oz) caster (superfine) sugar
100 ml (3½ fl oz) good-quality cognac
300 ml (10½ fl oz) thin (pouring/ whipping) cream
unsweetened cocoa powder or icing (confectioners') sugar, to serve

NOTES

The quality of the chocolate you use is directly proportional to the quality of the cake. This rule also applies to the cognac.

This cake rises like a soufflé, since that's really what it is. It will fall and set slowly in the oven as it cools, so don't be tempted to take it out too soon.

This cake will last for 3 days, covered, at room temperature. Don't refrigerate it: it will set like a brick!

Greek-style custard tart

SERVES 8–10

+ Using an electric mixer, beat the sugar and eggs until thick and pale, then add the semolina and combine well.

+ Add the milk and mix until smooth, then pour the mixture into a deep saucepan over medium heat. Bring to the boil, stirring continuously (hearty stirring is required), and cook for 2–3 minutes until the mixture thickens, then stir in the citrus zests. Remove from the heat, cover closely with plastic wrap and allow to cool.

+ Preheat the oven to 180°C (350°F/Gas 4).

+ Keeping the filo sheets covered while you work with one, lay a sheet on a large rectangular baking tray (see Note) and brush with melted butter. Place another sheet of filo on top and repeat brushing and layering until you have 7 sheets. Spoon the custard over the top, leaving a 3 cm (1¼ inch) border and place 7 remaining pastry sheets on top, buttering each as you go. Brush the top with butter, then roll in the edges to make a rectangular pie.

+ Bake the tart for 25–30 minutes or until the pastry is golden brown and crisp. Allow the tart to cool slightly, then sift icing sugar and cinnamon over the top. Cut into slices and serve warm.

400 g (14 oz) sugar
3 free-range eggs
275 g (9¾ oz/1½ cups) fine semolina
1.5 litres (52 fl oz/6 cups) milk
grated zest of 1 lemon
grated zest of 1 orange
500 g (1 lb 2 oz) filo pastry
   (you will need 14 sheets)
150 g (5½ oz) unsalted butter,
   melted
icing (confectioners') sugar and
   ground cinnamon, for dusting

NOTE

You will need a rectangular baking tray at least 42 cm (16½ inches) long. If you don't have one, then cut the filo sheets in half and make two smaller tarts.

Passionfruit and mandarin syllabub

SERVES 4

+ Place the mandarin zest and juice, passionfruit juice, sugar and wine in a bowl, then cover with plastic wrap and refrigerate overnight for the flavours to merge.

+ Using an electric mixer, slowly beat the chilled passionfruit mixture, then add the cream slowly. Watch the texture carefully — it should start to thicken and become light and cloud-like. Don't overbeat it or the cream will become grainy.

+ Spoon the syllabub into four chilled glasses or one large glass bowl. Place in the refrigerator for at least 1 hour before serving.

100 ml (3½ fl oz) strained passionfruit juice
zest and juice of 1 mandarin
75 g (2¾ oz/⅓ cup) caster (superfine) sugar
60 ml (2 fl oz/¼ cup) Muscat de Beaumes de Venise
400 ml (14 fl oz) thick (double/ heavy) cream

NOTE

Syllabub is an old-English-style dessert; it's basically wine-flavoured cream with ripe, soft fruit folded through. Many fruits will work, but I think passionfruit is perfect when in season. In late spring and summer, use puréed raspberries, cherries, peaches or mangoes.

Millefeuille of blueberries

An elegant dessert: light-as-air layers of puff pastry, cream and berries.

SERVES 4

+ For the pastry cream, using a hand-held whisk, beat the yolks and sugar in a bowl until pale and creamy. Sift in the flour and whisk until well combined.

+ Place the milk and vanilla bean and seeds in a heavy-based saucepan, and bring to the boil. Whisking continuously, slowly pour the hot milk mixture into the egg mixture, then pour the mixture back into the pan. Cook over low–medium heat, stirring continuously with a wooden spoon and bring to the boil. Cook for 5 minutes, stirring well, then transfer the custard to a bowl, cover closely with plastic wrap to prevent a skin from forming and set aside until cool, then refrigerate until chilled.

+ Roll out the pastry on a lightly floured work surface to 30 cm (12 inches) square — it should be about 3–5 mm (⅛–¼ inch) thick. Prick it all over with a fork, place on an oven tray and refrigerate for 2 hours.

+ Preheat the oven to 200°C (400°F/Gas 6). Bake the pastry for 30–40 minutes or until golden, puffed and dry. Remove from the oven and place on a wire rack. When cool, cut into 12 rectangles and store in an airtight container until needed.

+ To serve, whisk the cream to firm peaks. Fold a quarter of it into the cooled custard. Once it is well incorporated, gently fold in the rest of the cream.

+ Preheat the grill (broiler). Place the four best pastry pieces on a tray, sprinkle with icing sugar and grill until the sugar caramelises. Place a dot of pastry cream on each plate and top with another pastry piece. Add a dollop of pastry cream and a spoon of blueberries, then another pastry rectangle. Repeat, finishing with the glazed pastry.

NOTE

Any fruit can be used in millefeuille. Poach hard fruit such as apples or pears first, then slice. Summer fruit such as mangoes, peaches and figs are awesome.

350 g (12 oz) block store-bought puff pastry
plain (all-purpose) flour, for dusting
icing (confectioners') sugar, for dusting
2 x 125 g (4½ oz) punnets blueberries

Pastry cream

6 free-range egg yolks
130 g (4½ oz) caster (superfine) sugar
40 g (1½ oz) plain (all-purpose) flour
500 ml (17 fl oz/2 cups) milk
½ vanilla bean, split and seeds scraped
200 ml (7 fl oz) thin (pouring/whipping) cream

Summer celebration

For me, summer has always been about being outdoors, barbecues and lots of fresh Australian seafood. When it comes to dessert, throw that pudding out and celebrate all the wonderful fruit we have in season. This menu is all about prawns, tomatoes and fresh fruit. What could be more summery?

MENU SERVES 12

Pimm's from scratch

+ Combine all the ingredients, except the garnishes, in a small punch bowl or jug, with loads of ice. Finish with slices of cucumber, orange and lime, sprigs of mint and some summer berries.

+ This is, of course, the long and purist way round. By all means, grab a bottle of Pimm's and add equal parts of ginger ale and lemonade for the more common version of this, which I also love. Garnishes stay the same — mint and cucumber an absolute must at the very least.

+ The purist version is also not for the faint-hearted, so tread carefully.

360 ml (12½ fl oz) gin (Tanqueray is best)
180 ml (6 fl oz) sweet vermouth (Punt e Mes is ideal, but Martini Rosso will do)
60 ml (2 fl oz/¼ cup) Grand Marnier
12 dashes Angostura Bitters
6 thumb-sized knobs of ginger, peeled and finely grated
3 tablespoons light muscovado sugar
zest and juice of 3 lemons
1 litre (35 fl oz/4 cups) chilled Traditional Lemonade
1 litre (35 fl oz/4 cups) chilled sparkling water
cucumber, orange and lime slices and mint sprigs, to garnish
summer berries, to serve (optional)

King prawn salad with gazpacho salsa

+   For the salsa, remove the stalks from the tomatoes and plunge them into boiling water for about 10 seconds. Refresh in iced water and peel with a vegetable knife. Cut into quarters and remove the seeds. Cut the flesh into 2 cm (¾ inch) dice.

+   Finely chop the cucumbers, capsicums, chillies, garlic, onion and parsley. (I say finely chop, but you don't need to go crazy over this.) Place in a bowl with the tomato and remaining salsa ingredients and 125 ml (4 fl oz/½ cup) water and season with sea salt and black pepper to taste. Cover and refrigerate for at least 2 hours, but no longer than 4 hours.

+   When ready to serve, divide the lettuce among your serving bowls. Stack each bowl with 3 prawns and some gazpacho salsa, drizzle with extra virgin olive oil, and finish with a squeeze of lemon and a good grind of black pepper.

NOTES

Gazpacho is a rustic soup or salsa that goes well with any seafood you might serve at Christmas.

I have chosen prawns here, but if you really love your friends, you could buy cooked lobster, crabmeat or scallops.

You can cook whole salmon, kingfish or snapper instead, if you wish. Place it in the middle of the table with a green salad, potato salad or even more tomatoes, as they are amazing in the height of summer.

It is easy to grill (broil) a few bunches of asparagus and drizzle with extra virgin olive oil and lemon juice — perfect with the fish.

36 large cooked king prawns (shrimp) (or 1.2 kg/2 lb 10 oz cooked lobster meat), peeled and deveined
4 baby cos (romaine) lettuces, shredded
extra virgin olive oil, for drizzling
2 lemons

Salsa

1 kg (2 lb 4 oz) vine-ripened tomatoes
4 Lebanese (short) cucumbers, peeled, halved lengthways and seeded
4 red capsicums (peppers), halved and seeded
4 large fresh red chillies, halved lengthways and seeded
2 garlic cloves
2 small red onions
1 large handful flat-leaf (Italian) parsley leaves
80 ml (2½ fl oz/⅓ cup) red wine vinegar
60 ml (2 fl oz/¼ cup) extra virgin olive oil
Tabasco sauce, to taste
sea salt and freshly ground black pepper, to taste

Barbecued salmon cutlets with tomato vinaigrette

+ For the vinaigrette, remove the stalks from the tomatoes and plunge them into boiling water for about 10 seconds. Refresh in iced water and peel with a vegetable knife. Cut into quarters and remove the seeds. Cut the flesh into 2 cm (¾ inch) dice.

+ Mix the diced tomato with the rest of the vinaigrette ingredients in a bowl. Check the seasoning, then set aside for 1–2 hours for the flavours to mature. All the elements must get to mingle and start to have fun; it is then that the true quality of this sauce is revealed.

+ Preheat the barbecue to hot (make sure the grill bars are clean). Liberally sprinkle the cutlets with sea salt and brush with olive oil. Cook for 1 minute, then rotate the cutlets 90 degrees to create a perfect crisscross pattern on the fish, turn and repeat on the other side; the cutlets should take about 4 minutes in total to cook. The fish should be medium: don't overcook it unless you like it well done. Allow the fish to rest in a warm place for 2 minutes.

+ Place the cutlets neatly on a large plate, spoon about 375 ml (13 fl oz/1½ cups) vinaigrette over, add freshly ground black pepper and serve.

12 salmon cutlets
sea salt and freshly ground
    black pepper
extra virgin olive oil, for brushing

Tomato vinaigrette

6 vine-ripened tomatoes
2 garlic cloves, finely chopped
⅓ cup chopped chervil
⅓ cup chopped flat-leaf
    (Italian) parsley
2 tablespoons chopped tarragon
16 coriander seeds, crushed
300 ml (10½ fl oz) extra virgin
    olive oil

Summer stone fruit with pineapple granita

You can add a dollop of cream if you like but I don't think it's necessary.

+ For the granita, strain the pineapple juice through a fine sieve and place in a bowl with the sugar, mint and 250 ml (9 fl oz/ 1 cup) water. Stir for about 3 minutes until the sugar dissolves, then pour into a container that allows the mixture to be 5 cm (2 inches) deep. Place in the freezer. Using a fork, stir it every 30 minutes, scraping the edges and breaking up any chunks until the granita is slushy and frozen. This will take 4–5 hours.

+ Cut the peaches and nectarines from their stones and cut each half into pieces roughly the size of the cherries. Place the stone fruit in a bowl with the cherries, lemon juice and sugar. Toss well.

+ Divide the granita among 12 chilled glasses, top with the fruit, and serve.

> NOTE
>
> *Just about any fruit you can think of can make granita — the best are juicy fruits that have good flavour, so look at fruits that will go through a juice extractor and those that are very ripe.*

4 small–medium ripe peaches
  (slip-stone are best)
4 small–medium ripe nectarines
700 g (1 lb 9 oz) ripe, plump
  cherries, pitted
juice of 2 lemons
2 tablespoons caster (superfine) sugar

Granita

1 litre (35 fl oz/4 cups) freshly
  squeezed pineapple juice
230 g (8½ oz) caster (superfine) sugar
2 tablespoons finely chopped
  mint leaves

SHEET

EVENTS

RACE

The International Source for the History, Collection and

BOUR

We test drive the

FEATURE

Sunday

Bloody Mary and fried pizza with egg

I first had this at my dear friend Ronnie Di Stasio's country house. It was so simple but amazing. You will love the rich taste of the yolk as it breaks and mixes on the pizza base.

SERVES 4

+ Roll out each piece of dough to the size of a bread and butter plate.

+ Heat the olive oil in a frying pan a bit bigger than the dough over low–medium heat. Working one at a time, slide the pizza base in and cook for about 2 minutes, then turn over and carefully break an egg on top, being careful not to break the yolk. Now spoon the oil over the egg. Keep this up till the egg starts to set and at this stage the pizza base should be cooked.

+ Carefully remove the pizza with a fish slice, drain on paper towel then place on a plate, sprinkle with sea salt and lashings of freshly ground pepper. Serve and cook the remaining pizzas.

Pizza dough

+ Mix the honey and water together and warm to blood temperature. (Don't overheat the water or the yeast will die.) Add the yeast, crumbling it with your fingers. Stand for 10 minutes or until foamy.

+ Combine the flour with the salt in a large bowl, (this helps to dilute the salt as yeast hates it). Make a well in the centre then add the yeast mixture, after 10 minutes, add the olive oil to the flour. Mix the liquid into the flour. When it forms a mass, turn it out on to lightly floured work surface and knead. Continue kneading for 8 minutes until the dough is strong and elastic.

+ Place the dough back in the bowl, cover and allow it to prove in a warm place until the dough doubles in size, about 1 hour. At this stage it can be knocked down for use or refrigerated until needed (it must be allowed to come back to room temperature, usually a couple of hours, before use). Or freeze it.

Bloody Mary

SERVES 1

+ Place all the ingredients, except the celery stalk, in a cocktail shaker. Season to taste with salt and pepper and fill the shaker with ice. Roll the shaker forward and back three to four times to combine the ingredients.

+ Using a Hawthorne strainer, strain the liquid from the shaker into a glass filled with ice. Garnish with the celery stalk.

4 x 70 g (2½ oz) balls of pizza dough (see recipe below)
500 ml (17 fl oz/2 cups) olive oil
4 free-range or organic eggs
sea salt and freshly ground pepper

Pizza dough

750 g (1 lb 10 oz/5 cups) plain (all-purpose) flour, sifted
1 tablespoon sea salt
1½ tablespoons honey
500 ml (17 fl oz/2 cups) water
15 g (½ oz) fresh yeast
1¼ tablespoons extra virgin olive oil

Bloody Mary

50 ml (1½ fl oz) vodka
50 ml (1½ fl oz) tomato juice
20 ml (½ fl oz) carrot juice
20 ml (½ fl oz) celery juice
20 ml (½ fl oz) freshly squeezed lemon juice
2 teaspoons Worcestershire sauce
5 dashes red Tabasco sauce
5 dashes green Tabasco sauce
sea salt and freshly ground black pepper
1 small stalk celery, trimmed, to garnish

NOTES

This pizza dough is more than you need, but it works best in this volume, so make it and take what you need and freeze the rest.

Once the dough is made, form balls the size you want the pizzas and freeze like that.

Poached eggs with yoghurt, sage and chilli

These poached eggs show how simple yet complex and delicious an egg dish can be. Great any time of day.

SERVES 4

+ Combine the yoghurt and garlic in a bowl and season to taste with sea salt and black pepper. Place a large dollop in the centre of each of four plates. Spread it out, making a well in the middle for an egg.

+ Bring a large saucepan of water to the boil over high heat. Reduce the heat to low, then add the vinegar and a pinch of salt. Stir the water rapidly in one direction to create a whirlpool effect. One by one, break the eggs into a cup and slide them into the water (gently tip the cup near the water's surface).

+ When the eggs are cooked to your liking (3 minutes for a soft yolk), remove with a slotted spoon and drain on paper towel. Place an egg in the middle of each plate. Season with salt and pepper and sprinkle with chilli flakes.

+ Heat a frying pan over medium–high heat. Add the butter and sage and cook, shaking the pan often, for about 2 minutes until the butter turns nut brown and the sage is crisp. Remove from the heat and spoon the butter and sage leaves over the yoghurt and eggs. Serve immediately.

4 very fresh free-range
   or organic eggs
350 g (12 oz) Greek-style yoghurt
1 garlic clove, crushed to a paste
   with a pinch of salt
sea salt and freshly ground
   black pepper
2 teaspoons white wine vinegar
1 teaspoon mild chilli flakes
100 g (3½ oz) butter
1 small bunch sage, leaves picked

NOTE

It is important to use thick, Greek-style yoghurt for the eggs — think sour! Commercial, sweet-tasting yoghurt will kill the whole deal.

Hummus with ground beef and pine nuts

Fill the table with Mediterranean flavours. Just add a salad or zesty tabouleh, with rice or pitta bread.

SERVES 4

+ Heat 60 ml (2 fl oz/¼ cup) of the olive oil in a saucepan over low–medium heat. Add the onion and cook gently for about 5 minutes until golden brown. Transfer to a bowl, add the cinnamon and set aside.

+ To make the hummus, place the chickpeas and 60 ml (2 fl oz/¼ cup) water in a food processor and blend until smooth. Add the juice of 1 lemon, the garlic paste, tahini and remaining olive oil. Season to taste with sea salt and black pepper. Spread the hummus over a large serving plate.

+ Place a frying pan over high heat. When the pan is hot, add the cooked onion, then the beef mince. Use the back of a fork to break up the mince as it cooks and season with salt. Cook for about 10 minutes until the mince begins to crisp, then add the pine nuts.

+ To serve, spoon the mince over the hummus, and sprinkle with the parsley, paprika and chilli flakes. Add a good grind of pepper and squeeze the juice of the remaining lemon over the top. Serve with lemon wedges and toasted pitta bread.

250 g (9 oz) good-quality minced (ground) beef
125 ml (4 fl oz/½ cup) extra virgin olive oil
½ large red onion, very finely diced
⅓ teaspoon ground cinnamon
400 g (14 oz) tin chickpeas, drained and rinsed
2 lemons, plus extra wedges, to serve
2–3 garlic cloves, crushed to a paste with salt
135 g (4¾ oz/½ cup) tahini paste
sea salt and freshly ground black pepper
2 tablespoons pine nuts, toasted
½ cup flat-leaf (Italian) parsley leaves, shredded
paprika and mild chilli flakes, to taste
toasted pitta bread, to serve

Smoked salmon with poached eggs

When poaching, more than any other type of cooking with eggs, fresh is best. Other smoked fish like hot smoked trout or sturgeon are great with this little brunch dish.

SERVES 4

+ Bring a saucepan of salted water to the simmer. Don't have your saucepan filled too deeply with water, no deeper than about 4 cm (1½ inches). Don't have the water boiling too fiercely or your eggs will blow apart, just barely simmering is perfect. Don't try to cook too many eggs at one time. As you become more proficient, you can be a little bolder and fill the pan.

+ One by one, break the eggs into a cup and slide them into the water (gently tip the cup near the water's surface). Gently spoon water from the pan over the eggs as they cook. This helps to cook the tops so you don't have to turn them over.

+ Carefully remove the eggs with a slotted spoon when set to your liking. Drain on paper towel.

+ In the meantime, toast the bread. Place 3 slices of smoked salmon on each plate. Make sure there is a little space for the egg to fit in the middle, so build a little nest really. Place a poached egg on each pile, drizzle with olive oil, squeeze lemon juice over the salmon and season with sea salt and black pepper.

12 slices of smoked salmon
4 free-range or organic eggs
sourdough or Turkish bread,
    toasted
sea salt and freshly ground
    pepper
extra virgin olive oil
1 lemon

NOTES

Break each egg into a cup, it is easier to slide into the water than breaking directly into a pan.

Some cos (romaine) lettuce lightly dressed with olive oil and lemon juice is a nice addition under the salmon too.

Pancake stack

These buttermilk pancakes are great with any berries, but also nice with ripe stone fruit. They are yummy with a whipped maple syrup butter on them, or even just plain maple syrup poured straight over.

SERVES 4–6

150 g (5½ oz/1 cup) plain (all-purpose) flour
2 tablespoons caster (superfine) sugar
2 teaspoons baking powder
1 teaspoon bicarbonate of soda (baking soda)
½ teaspoon salt
½ teaspoon ground cinnamon
2 free-range eggs
375 ml (13 fl oz/1½ cups) buttermilk
125 g (4½ oz) fresh ricotta cheese
160 g (5¾ oz) unsalted butter, melted and cooled
yoghurt and fresh berries, to serve

+ Sift the flour, sugar, baking powder, bicarbonate of soda, salt and cinnamon into a large bowl. Break the eggs into a bowl and lightly beat with a fork. Add the buttermilk and ricotta to the eggs and beat well. Add the buttermilk mixture to the flour mixture and stir to combine, then stir in half the melted butter.

+ Heat a large, heavy-based frying pan over medium heat and add a little of the remaining butter to the pan. Make 2 or 3 pancakes at a time by pouring batter into the pan, leaving space between each one, so they don't join. Cook until bubbles form and the bottoms are golden, this takes about 2 minutes.

+ Turn the pancakes and continue cooking for another 2 minutes, or until they are cooked through.

+ Repeat the process, adding a little more butter to the pan each time, and keeping the pancakes warm in the oven on low while you cook the remainder.

+ Serve immediately with yoghurt and some beautiful fresh berries.

Zucchini frittata

This frittata is great for supper or a light lunch with a salad.
You can vary it by adding other vegetables like asparagus
or even a dollop of cheese such as ricotta.

SERVES 6

+ Preheat the oven to 200°C (400°F/Gas 6).

+ Trim the zucchini, then thinly slice on the diagonal (about 1 cm/
  ½ inch thick).

+ Heat 2 tablespoons of the olive oil in an ovenproof frying pan
  over medium heat. Add the garlic followed by the zucchini slices
  and cook until the zucchini is brown on both sides. Add a third
  of the basil and season with sea salt and pepper to taste. The
  zucchini should be quite dry; if there is any oil remaining, drain
  through a sieve and reserve.

+ Break the eggs into a bowl and lightly beat with a fork. Add half
  of the garlic and zucchini mixture, reserving the other half for
  the end. Season with salt and pepper.

+ Heat the remaining oil in an ovenproof, non-stick frying pan over
  a medium heat. Add the egg mixture and cook, moving the egg
  off the base of the pan with a spatula, until it resembles runny
  scrambled eggs. Place the remaining zucchini slices on the top
  and place into the oven. When the egg is just set, remove from
  the oven and sprinkle with the parmesan and remaining basil.

+ Place a plate over the frying pan and carefully invert the frittata
  onto the plate. Serve warm or at room temperature.

3 zucchini (courgettes)
60 ml (2 fl oz/¼ cup) olive oil
2 garlic cloves, finely chopped
1 small bunch basil, leaves picked
  and roughly chopped
sea salt and freshly ground pepper
8 free-range eggs
50 g (1¾ oz/⅓ cup) finely grated
  parmesan

Calf's liver, bacon and tomato

This is a dish from my childhood. My father, being a butcher, loved all parts of the animal so Sunday breakfast would often be lamb's fry (liver) or calf's liver with bacon and tomato. We had quite a love of kidneys too! And OK, so you may not think bacon fat is good for you, but you don't eat it every day and when you do, you need to celebrate how delicious it is. When the bacon dressing meets the tomato juices on the toast … heaven!

SERVES 4

400 g (14 oz) calves liver, skinned
  and thinly sliced
8 rashers quality smoked bacon
4 vine-ripened tomatoes
2 tablespoons extra virgin olive oil
sea salt and freshly ground pepper
4 slices of sourdough bread or
  4 long slices of baguette, cut
  on the diagonal

+   Preheat the oven to 150°C (300°F/Gas 2).

+   Using a paring knife, remove the core from each of the tomatoes. Cut in half through the 'equator' and put in a roasting tin, cut side down. Drizzle the extra virgin olive oil over the tomatoes, sprinkle with sea salt and roast for 1½ hours, then remove and pull the skin away with a pair of tongs — it should come away easily (I usually use my fingers, but it depends on how tough you are), season with a grind of fresh pepper.

+   Place the bacon in a non-stick frying pan over medium heat. After about 5 minutes as the bacon fat melts and lubricates the pan, turn the heat up and cook the bacon till crisp. Remove and dry on paper towel.

+   Season the liver with sea salt and remove half the bacon fat from the pan. Over high heat, cook the liver in the bacon fat quickly on both sides, you want a nice crust on the outside and a tender medium texture in the middle.

+   Toast the bread and place in the centre of four plates. Place 2 tomato halves on each piece of toast, spoon the juices over, put the bacon on top and then top the tomato with liver, pour the pan juices over and give a good grind of pepper. Serve immediately.

Sweet corn soup with garlic and chipotle butter

This soup is delicious with crabmeat or cooked king prawns (shrimp) through it (in which case forget the butter). I also like chopped chicken meat and an egg beaten through at the end, a Western version of my favourite chicken and sweet corn soup in Chinese restaurants.

SERVES 4–6

+ For the garlic and chipotle butter, process all the ingredients in a food processor until just combined. Season to taste, then roll the mixture in a sheet of baking paper into a log about 20 cm (8 inches) long and 4 cm (1½ inches) in diameter. Wrap in plastic wrap, refrigerate until firm or freeze for later use.

+ Heat the olive oil and butter in a heavy-based saucepan over low heat. Add the onion, garlic, ginger and a pinch of sea salt, then cook slowly for 6–8 minutes or until the onion is very soft. Add the corn kernels and chicken stock and simmer, covered, for about 25 minutes or until the corn is very tender. Purée the soup in a food processor until smooth.

+ While you are making the soup, remove the butter from the refrigerator and allow it to come near to room temperature.

+ Divide the soup between serving bowls, add a spoonful of the garlic and chipotle butter and give a good grind of white pepper. I'm also fond of a good drizzle of extra virgin olive oil at this stage. Serve.

900 g (2 lb) corn kernels, scraped off the cob (you will need about 5 cobs)
1 tablespoon olive oil
40 g (1½ oz) unsalted butter
1 brown onion, diced
2 garlic cloves, finely chopped
1 small knob of ginger (about 20 g/¾ oz), peeled and finely chopped
1.5 litres (52 fl oz/6 cups) chicken stock
extra virgin olive oil, for drizzling

Garlic and chipotle butter

200 g (7 oz) unsalted butter, softened
1 small knob of ginger, peeled and finely chopped
1 small handful flat-leaf (Italian) parsley, finely chopped
1 tablespoon chipotle chilli powder
squeeze of lemon juice
sea salt and freshly ground white pepper

NOTES

Like all compound butters the garlic and chipotle is good left in the freezer and will be perfect with any pan-fried or roasted fish or meat.

If you don't have chipotle just use chilli flakes, it will be spicy, but lack the smokiness that chipotle brings.

Corn on the cob with cheese and lime

This is a classic combination of cheese, chilli and lime that you see in a lot of Mexican food. When mixed with the sweet flavour of the corn it is a killer dish.

SERVES 4

4 cobs corn, in the husk
olive oil, for brushing
60 g (2¼ oz/¼ cup) mayonnaise

pinch of cayenne pepper
100 g (3½ oz/⅔ cup) finely crumbled feta,
lime wedges, to serve

+ Preheat a charcoal or gas grill.

+ Pull the husks back from the corn, leaving them attached at the base, then remove and discard the silks. Wrap the husks back around the cobs and soak in water for 10 minutes. Drain well.

+ Lightly oil the grill. Grill the corn, turning occasionally to brown evenly, for about 10 minutes. Carefully pull back the husks and grill for another 5 minutes or until the kernels are browned and tender.

+ Meanwhile, whisk together the mayonnaise and cayenne pepper in a bowl.

+ Brush the mayonnaise onto the hot corn, then sprinkle with the crumbled feta and serve with lime wedges.

Salad of asparagus and soft-boiled egg vinaigrette

This salad in summer benefits from a few ripe cherry tomatoes tossed through it and is awesome with some sliced buffalo mozzarella or burrata. This is my go-to salad in season.

SERVES 4

+ Break off the dry ends of the asparagus. Fill a large saucepan with water, salt it until it tastes like the sea, and bring to the boil. Blanch the asparagus for 3–5 minutes depending on the thickness of the spears. Drain and immerse in iced water. As soon as they are cool, drain and pat dry on paper towel.

+ Bring another saucepan of water to the boil and salt it well. Place the eggs in and cook for exactly 6 minutes, then drain and run under cold water or place in iced water until cold. Gently crack the shells with a spoon and leave soaking in the cold water for 10 minutes, then peel.

+ Meanwhile, place the shallots and red wine vinegar in a bowl together, leave for 10 minutes then whisk in the olive oil and season to taste.

+ Place a pile of asparagus lengthways in the middle of each of four plates, cut the eggs in half carefully (they will have a soft centre), place the halves on and about the asparagus, drizzle with the vinaigrette, give a good grind of white pepper and scatter with shaved parmesan.

2 bunches green asparagus
4 x 55 g (2 oz) free-range eggs
2 small red Asian shallots, finely chopped
2 tablespoons red wine vinegar
125 ml (4 fl oz/½ cup) extra virgin olive oil
sea salt and freshly ground white pepper
shaved parmesan, to serve

NOTES

Trust me, yes, the egg needs 6 minutes, but must be chilled quickly. Soaking the egg helps water get between the shell and egg and makes peeling easier, so does peeling under running water.

Make sure the asparagus is removed from the iced water the moment it is chilled. Soaking too long makes it taste more and more like water.

Moroccan lamb soup

This is a hearty spicy delicious soup that is perfect in winter. It is also great served with some couscous. If you aren't sold on legumes then replace them with cooked rice.

SERVES 4

+ Heat the olive oil in a heavy-based saucepan over high heat. Brown the lamb lightly, then add the chermoula and cook for 5 minutes. Add the tomato and chicken stock and season to taste with sea salt. Reduce the heat to as low as possible, cover and cook for 1½ hours or until tender.

+ When the meat is tender, add the honey, beans and lentils and stir for 1–2 minutes or until heated through. Remove one-third of the soup and purée in a blender until smooth, then return the purée to the soup in the pan. Check the seasoning, then divide among four bowls, drizzle with extra virgin olive oil and squeeze the juice of a lemon quarter into each.

400 g (14 oz) trimmed boneless
  lamb shoulder, cut into 1 cm
  (½ inch) cubes
2 tablespoons olive oil
1 quantity chermoula (see page 121)
4 ripe tomatoes, roughly chopped
1.5 litres (52 fl oz/6 cups) chicken
  stock or water
sea salt
2 tablespoons honey
100 g (3½ oz/½ cup) drained and
  rinsed tinned butter beans
  (see Notes)
100 g (3½ oz/½ cup) drained and
  rinsed tinned red lentils
extra virgin olive oil, for drizzling
1 lemon, cut into quarters

NOTES

If you have dried lentils and butter beans on hand, then simply bring them to the boil, rinse and then return them to the saucepan, add water and salt and simmer until tender. You will need to cook them separately, of course, as they will take different times to become tender.

Boiling the legumes first takes away the need to soak overnight. However the tinned products are so good and simple to use I would suggest taking the short cut every time.

Use whatever beans you like — I also love using borlotti, amongst others.

Spicy salmon salad

Start this recipe five hours before you intend to serve it.

SERVES 4 AS PART OF A SHARED BANQUET

+ To make the marinade, combine all the ingredients in a bowl. Add the salmon, turn to coat well, then cover and refrigerate for 3 hours. Remove from the refrigerator and stand for 2 hours to allow it to come closer to room temperature before cooking.

+ To make the dressing, pound the lemongrass, chillies, garlic and sugar in a mortar and pestle until a fine paste forms. Add the fish sauce and lime juice and taste for balance.

+ Heat a grill (broiler) or barbecue to hot, wipe off excess marinade and cook the salmon for about 4 minutes on each side or until it forms an even crust and the flesh can be flaked. Set aside in a warm place to rest for 5 minutes.

+ Flake the salmon into a bowl. Add the red onion, coriander, spring onions and a little of the dressing. Arrange the lettuce and salmon mix on a serving plate and drizzle with the remaining dressing. Sprinkle with ground roast rice, crushed peanuts and a good grind of black pepper.

> *NOTE*
>
> *Ground roast rice adds great texture to many dishes. Simply toast jasmine rice in a dry, heavy-based frying pan over low heat until each grain is opaque but not coloured. When cool, grind it into a coarse powder using a mortar and pestle or, for ease, a spice grinder.*

400 g (14 oz) salmon fillet, pin-boned and skin removed
1 small red onion, thinly sliced
1 small handful coriander (cilantro) leaves
2 spring onions (scallions), cut into julienne, the green part as well as the white
1 small butter lettuce, leaves separated
pinch of ground roast rice (see Note)
2 tablespoons roasted peanuts, crushed
freshly ground black pepper

Marinade

2 tablespoons oyster sauce
1 tablespoon fish sauce
1 tablespoon grated palm sugar (jaggery)
½ teaspoon sesame oil

Dressing

1 lemongrass stem, tough outer leaves removed, chopped
1 long fresh red chilli, seeded and chopped
2 small green scud chillies, chopped
3 garlic cloves, chopped
1 tablespoon caster (superfine) sugar
2 tablespoons fish sauce
juice of 3 limes

Salad of Roquefort, pears, walnuts, radicchio and witlof

This salad is an awesome little starter, or something that sits nicely as a side dish beside a steak. It is a classic combo of salty, creamy, pungent cheese with the sweet juiciness of pears, the crunch and deep flavour of the nuts all carried by the bitter leaves. I personally love it and it's easy to see why it is a classic.

SERVES 4

+ Preheat the oven to 240°C (475°F/Gas 8).

+ Place the onion wedges on a baking tray, drizzle with a little olive oil, season with sea salt and roast for 25 minutes or until soft and caramelised.

+ Tear the witlof leaves in half and the radicchio leaves into smaller pieces. Place all the leaves in a bowl, add the juice of 1 lemon, drizzle with extra virgin olive oil and season to taste. Toss gently.

+ Quarter and core the pears, then cut each quarter lengthways into thirds. Place the pear pieces in a bowl and gently toss with the juice of half of the remaining lemon to stop the pears from browning.

+ Divide the leaves among four large plates, then scatter with roast onion, pear, Roquefort and walnuts. Drizzle each salad with a little extra oil and squeeze over some lemon juice as well. Give a last grind of white pepper and serve.

150 g (5½ oz) Roquefort cheese, crumbled
2 red onions, each cut into 6 wedges
extra virgin olive oil, for drizzling
sea salt and freshly ground white pepper
1 witlof (chicory/Belgian endive), leaves separated
1 radicchio, outer leaves discarded
2 lemons
2 firm ripe pears
80 g (2¾ oz/⅔ cup) walnuts, roasted and broken into rough pieces

Lamb and macaroni bake

Inspired by the Greek dish pastitsio, this bake can be made with lamb or beef. It turns simple ingredients into something very tasty.

SERVES 8

+ Preheat the oven to 200°C (400°F/Gas 6).

+ For the lamb sauce, heat the olive oil in a heavy-based saucepan over low heat. Add the onion and a good pinch of sea salt and cook, stirring regularly, for 15 minutes or until soft.

+ Add the lamb, increase the heat to high and cook until browned, breaking up any lumps with a wooden spoon. Add the tomato, bay leaf and enough water to cover and simmer for 30 minutes or until the water has evaporated and the meat is tender. Season to taste.

+ Meanwhile, for the béchamel, melt the butter in a saucepan over medium heat. When foaming, stir in the flour and stir for 1 minute or until the mixture looks sandy. Stirring continuously, gradually add the warm milk and cook until the sauce thickens. Remove from the heat, then beat in the eggs and Gruyère and season to taste with nutmeg, salt and pepper.

+ Place the cooked macaroni and one-third of the bechamel in a bowl and combine well.

+ Place half the macaroni mixture into an ovenproof dish measuring 23 x 29 x 7 cm (9 x 11½ x 2¾ inch). Add the lamb sauce, then top with the remaining macaroni. Mix half the cheeses with the remaining béchamel and pour over the macaroni, then sprinkle the remaining cheeses on top. Bake for 20–30 minutes or until browned on top. Remove from the oven and allow to rest for 10 minutes before serving.

500 g (1 lb 2 oz) macaroni, cooked until *al dente*, drained and tossed in a little olive oil
200 g (7 oz/2 cups) grated Gruyère
50 g (1¾ oz/½ cup) grated parmesan

Lamb sauce

500 g (1 lb 2 oz) minced (ground) lamb
100 ml (3½ fl oz) extra virgin olive oil
2 large onions, finely chopped
sea salt and freshly ground white pepper
2–3 tomatoes, peeled, seeded and then diced (or you can use 400 g/ 14 oz tin diced tomatoes)
1 bay leaf

Béchamel sauce

60 g (2¼ oz) butter
75 g (2¾ oz/½ cup) plain (all-purpose) flour
750 ml (26 fl oz/3 cups) warm milk
3 free-range eggs, lightly beaten
100 g (3½ oz/1 cup) grated Gruyère
freshly grated nutmeg, to taste

NOTE

If you have a favourite bolognese recipe, use that instead of the lamb sauce, add the béchamel and pasta, and you will end up with a great treat.

Green lentil curry with spinach

SERVES 4

+ Place the lentils in a saucepan, cover with cold water and bring to the boil. Drain immediately and rinse.

+ Place the blanched lentils, turmeric, bay leaf and 1 litre (35 fl oz/ 4 cups) water in a heavy-based saucepan with a tight-fitting lid over medium heat. Stir and bring to a simmer. Reduce the heat to low, cover, and cook gently for about 1 hour or until the lentils are tender.

+ Add the spinach, sea salt, chilli powder, cumin and 80 ml (2½ oz/ ⅓ cup) water. Stir to combine, then return to a simmer. Cover and simmer gently for 30 minutes, stirring from time to time. Stir in the fresh chillies, remove the bay leaf and serve with steamed rice.

215 g (7½ oz/1 cup) green lentils
½ teaspoon ground turmeric
1 bay leaf
1 bunch spinach, leaves picked, washed well and shredded
1 teaspoon sea salt
½ teaspoon red chilli powder
1 teaspoon cumin seeds, toasted and lightly crushed
2 fresh red chillies, cut into thin rounds
steamed rice, to serve

NOTE

Bringing the lentils to the boil as a first stand-alone point relieves the need to soak them. This also helps the lentils to hold their shape during cooking. All pulses can be treated in this way. Be aware though that different types of lentils will differ in their cooking times, so it is always wise to check the packet instructions and test along the way.

Crispy blue-eye trevalla marinated in red bean curd

This dish is also a great idea as a finger food — with a squeeze of fresh lemon.

SERVES 2, OR 4 AS PART OF A SHARED BANQUET

+ To make the marinade, place all the ingredients in a bowl and combine well.

+ Add the blue-eye to the marinade and toss until well coated, then set aside for 30 minutes.

+ Fill a wok or deep-fryer two-thirds full of oil, or to the fill line over medium–high heat until just starting to smoke, about 180°C (350°F).

+ Remove the fish from the marinade and dust with the tapioca flour, shaking off any excess. Deep-fry the fish, in batches until golden brown, then remove and drain on paper towel.

+ Serve on a bed of mixed lettuce leaves, with lemon wedges on the side, and a bowl of steamed rice if desired.

350 g (12 oz) skinless blue-eye trevalla fillet, cut into bite-sized pieces
vegetable oil, for deep-frying
80 g (2¾ oz/½ cup) tapioca flour
mixed lettuce leaves, lemon wedges and steamed rice, to serve

Marinade

2 tablespoons fermented red bean curd, mashed (see Notes)
1 tablespoon store-bought bean curd marinade (available from Asian grocers)
2 tablespoons Shaoxing rice wine
½ teaspoon Chinese five-spice
2 garlic cloves, finely chopped

NOTES

Fermented red bean curd is a pungent flavouring agent made from bean curd cubes, which have a gamey aroma. It is available at good Asian grocers.

The red bean curd marinade is great with other fish, and prawns or scallops, too. It's also fab on quail and chicken, and with anything off the barbecue. Here, the crispy blue-eye is served with mixed lettuce leaves, but blanched broccoli works just as well.

Grilled snapper fillet with spiced sweet potato salad and yoghurt

It goes without saying that any white fish is great here. However I really believe that this dish is suited to a fish like mackerel or trevally, inexpensive and very sustainable, the wonderful oiliness goes perfectly with the spice.

SERVES 4

+   For the sweet potato salad, place the sweet potatoes in a large saucepan and cover completely with water. Bring to the boil, season with sea salt and cook until the sweet potatoes are tender. Carefully drain, then place on a paper towel-lined plate.

+   Heat half the olive oil in a large frying pan over low–medium heat. Cook the onion for 5 minutes or until translucent then add the sweet potato, spices and a little salt and toss to incorporate. Add the remaining oil, the lemon juice, olives and parsley and toss again until evenly mixed. Remove from the heat and allow to cool.

+   Preheat a grill (broiler) or frying pan to hot. Season the fish fillets with sea salt and drizzle with a little olive oil. Place the fish onto the grill skin side down and cook for 3 minutes without moving, then turn over and cook for another 2 minutes or until just cooked through.

+   Place the yoghurt and a little lemon juice in a small bowl, season to taste and combine well.

+   Serve the fish topped with a dollop of the yoghurt, with the sweet potato salad and lemon cheeks to the side.

4 snapper fillets, about 200 g
    (7 oz) each, skin on
sea salt and freshly ground
    white pepper
olive oil, for drizzling
1 lemon, quartered
260 g (1 cup) Greek-style yoghurt
squeeze of lemon, plus cheeks,
    to serve

Sweet potato salad

500 g (1 lb 2 oz) sweet potato,
    peeled and cut into 2 cm
    (¾ inch) dice
125 ml (4 fl oz/½ cup) extra virgin
    olive oil
1 large onion, roughly chopped
½ teaspoon ground ginger
½ teaspoon ground cumin
½ teaspoon paprika
½ teaspoon chilli powder
juice of ½ lemon
12 green olives, pitted and
    roughly chopped
¼ cup flat-leaf (Italian) parsley,
    finely shredded

NOTE

The cooking times will vary depending on the thickness of the fish. Just try to cook it on the skin side longer and make sure you don't overcook it.

Braised chicken with peas and red wine and soft polenta

You can make this classic braise with any meat or poultry. I have sometimes added mussels to the base for a wonderful, generous dish. I also love this dish with tinned white beans instead of peas. Just fold them through and simmer until warm. They're creamy and delicious.

SERVES 4

+ Preheat the oven to 160°C (315°F/Gas 2–3).

+ Season the chicken with sea salt. Heat the olive oil in a large, heavy-based ovenproof saucepan with a tight-fitting lid over high heat. Cook the chicken, in batches, skin side down first until golden. Remove from the pan and set aside.

+ Reduce the heat to medium, then add the onion, garlic, ginger, rosemary, thyme, chilli and carrot to the pan and stir for 2 minutes or until starting to soften. Add the wine and simmer until reduced by half. Add the tomatoes, chicken stock and chicken. Season to taste and bring to the boil. Cover with the lid and bake for 20 minutes or until just cooked.

+ Meanwhile, for the polenta, bring 1.125 litres (39 fl oz/4½ cups) water to the boil in a saucepan. Add some sea salt and slowly pour in the polenta, whisking continuously, until it is completely incorporated. Reduce the heat to low and simmer gently for 40 minutes, stirring with a wooden spoon from time to time, until the polenta loses its graininess. Stir in the butter and parmesan, then season to taste. Transfer the polenta to a serving dish and sprinkle with extra parmesan and a grind of pepper.

+ Transfer the chicken in the pan, uncovered, to the stovetop and bring the sauce to a gentle, rolling simmer. Add the peas and cook for a further 5 minutes. Check the seasoning and adjust if necessary.

+ Divide the chicken, vegetables and sauce among four bowls and top with a generous grind of pepper. Serve with soft polenta or small pasta such as risoni.

8 free-range chicken thighs (organic if possible), bone in and skin on
sea salt and freshly ground white pepper
60 ml (2 fl oz/¼ cup) extra virgin olive oil
1 red onion, sliced
8 garlic cloves, crushed
1 tablespoon julienned ginger
2 rosemary sprigs
4 thyme sprigs
2 long dried red chillies, seeds removed, crushed
2 carrots, sliced into 1 cm (½ inch) rounds
250 ml (9 fl oz/1 cup) good-quality red wine
400 g (14 oz) tin tomatoes
150 ml (5 fl oz) chicken stock
420 g (14¾ oz/3 cups) frozen peas
soft polenta (see recipe below) or risoni, to serve

Soft polenta

250 g (9 oz) good-quality polenta
sea salt and freshly ground white pepper
100 g (3½ oz) unsalted butter, chopped
150 g (5½ oz) finely grated parmesan, plus extra, to serve

NOTES

Frozen peas are sweet and so easy — no shelling. They give the chicken braise a sweetness.

You can serve soft polenta as an entrée, too. Add a pasta sauce to it and a sprinkle of freshly grated parmesan.

I love sautéing mushrooms until caramelised and serving them on soft polenta, with a mild cheese such as fontina folded through.

Roast chook with kumara and ginger purée

If you start with a really good tasting bird and look after it, roast chicken is a dish fit for a king.

SERVES 4

+ Take the chicken out of the refrigerator 2 hours before cooking.

+ Preheat the oven to 160°C (315°F/Gas 2–3). Season the chicken inside and out with sea salt. Cut 1 lemon in half, squeeze a little juice into the cavity of the bird, then place the 2 lemon halves and the parsley sprigs in the cavity. Truss the chicken (see Note), and rub it all over with the olive oil.

+ Place the chicken on its side in a heavy-based roasting tin and roast for 20 minutes. Turn the bird onto its other side and roast for another 20 minutes. Turn it onto its back and roast it for a further 20 minutes or until cooked.

+ Turn the oven down to 60°C (140°F/Gas ¼) and open the door for a few minutes to let out the heat. Allow the chicken to rest for 15 minutes in the warm oven.

+ Meanwhile for the kumara and ginger purée, place the kumara, ginger and sea salt in a saucepan and add enough cold water so the vegetables are not quite covered. Bring to the boil over medium–high heat. Reduce the heat to low and simmer gently for about 20 minutes or until soft. Add the butter, then purée with a food processor or hand-held blender until smooth. Check the seasoning and finish with extra butter and a good grind of white pepper.

+ To carve the chicken, remove the string and pull the legs apart, run a sharp knife down and through the hip bone, removing the legs; separate the drumstick and thigh at the joint. Remove the breasts with the winglet. Cut each breast in half lengthways.

+ To serve, place a dollop of kumara and ginger purée on each plate and top with chicken. Drizzle with extra olive oil, then add a squeeze of lemon, a grind of white pepper and a sprinkle of crushed sea salt. Serve immediately with a lightly dressed green salad.

2 kg (4 lb 8 oz) whole free-range chicken (organic if possible)
sea salt and freshly ground white pepper
1½ lemons
a few flat-leaf (Italian) parsley sprigs
80 ml (2½ fl oz/⅓ cup) extra virgin olive oil, plus extra, for drizzling
green salad, to serve

Kumara and ginger purée

500 g (1 lb 2 oz) kumara (sweet potato), peeled and cut into 2–3 cm (¾–1¼ inch) dice
2 tablespoons chopped ginger
2 tablespoons sea salt
100 g (3½ oz) unsalted butter, diced, plus extra, to finish
freshly ground white pepper

NOTES

By all means, squeeze some lemon into the pan juices and whisk in a little butter. Pour this over the chicken to make a simple, tasty sauce.

For instructions on trussing a chook see Note page 10.

Yoghurt-marinated chicken with tomato salsa

Marinated chicken, ripe tomatoes and rice are a combo made in heaven. The marinade is also perfect with fish — try blue-eye trevalla, snapper or ocean trout.

SERVES 4

+   For the marinade, combine all the ingredients in a bowl.

+   Add the chicken breasts to the marinade, combine well, cover with plastic wrap and marinate in the refrigerator for 2 hours.

+   Place the tomatoes in a bowl and sprinkle with sea salt. After about 10 minutes, add the extra virgin olive oil, vinegar and a good grind of black pepper and toss to combine.

+   Heat a barbecue until smoking hot (if you don't have a barbecue, use a frying pan or grill plate on the stovetop). Cook the chicken, skin side down, for about 5 minutes, then turn and cook for a further 5 minutes. Set aside in a warm place to rest for 10 minutes.

+   Place a good amount of tomato salsa on four plates, then top each with a chicken breast (if you want to impress, carve it lengthways). Add a squeeze of lemon juice and a good grind of pepper. Serve with a pan of rice pilaf (see recipe, below) in the middle of the table and a green salad.

4 free-range chicken breasts (organic if possible), skin on and winglets attached
250 g (9 oz) red and yellow cherry tomatoes, halved
sea salt and freshly ground white pepper
80 ml (2½ fl oz/⅓ cup) extra virgin olive oil
2 tablespoons red wine vinegar
1 lemon
green salad, to serve

Marinade

2 garlic cloves, crushed
½ red onion, finely grated
juice and grated zest of ½ lemon
1 teaspoon sweet paprika
½ teaspoon chilli powder
2 teaspoons cumin seeds, coarsely ground
¼ cup roughly chopped coriander (cilantro) leaves
150 g (5½ oz) good-quality sheep's milk yoghurt
60 ml (2 fl oz/¼ cup) olive oil
freshly ground black pepper

Rice pilaf

SERVES 4

+   Heat the butter and olive oil over medium heat in a saucepan with a tight-fitting lid that's just large enough to fit the rice and stock. When the butter foams, add the cinnamon and sea salt, then add the onion and cook, stirring occasionally for 10 minutes or until the onion is soft and starting to colour. Don't brown heavily. Add the cardamom, turmeric, currants and pistachios and cook gently for 10 minutes, until the onion is golden brown.

+   Drain the rice, add to the pan and stir for 1–2 minutes to coat all the grains — this keeps each grain separate — then pour in the stock. Cover with the lid and cook over high heat for 5 minutes until it boils. Reduce the heat to low and simmer for 10 minutes.

+   Remove from the heat and allow the pilaf to rest, covered for 10 minutes. Serve directly onto plates or place the pan in the middle of the table so your guests can help themselves.

60 g (2¼ oz) unsalted butter
2 tablespoons olive oil
2 cinnamon sticks
1 teaspoon fine sea salt
1 large red onion, thinly sliced
½ teaspoon ground cardamom
1 teaspoon ground turmeric
2 tablespoons currants
30 g (1 oz/¼ cup) unsalted pistachios
300 g (10½ oz) basmati rice, soaked in water for 1 hour
500 ml (17 fl oz/2 cups) chicken stock or water

Slow-roasted shoulder of lamb

This dish is so sublime — it is equally good simply served with great bread and butter. Start this recipe the night before.

SERVES 4–6

2 lamb shoulders on the bone, about
   1.25kg–1.5kg (2 lb 12 oz–3 lb 5 oz) each
½ teaspoon ground coriander
½ teaspoon ground fennel
½ teaspoon ground cinnamon
2 star anise, ground

¼ teaspoon ground cardamom
2 teaspoons sea salt
freshly ground white pepper
60 ml (2 fl oz/¼ cup) extra virgin
   olive oil, plus extra, for drizzling
lemon wedges, to serve

+ The night before serving, trim the excess fat from the edges of the lamb shoulders. Mix the spices, sea salt, white pepper and olive oil together, and rub over the lamb. Place the lamb in a container, loosely cover with plastic wrap, then refrigerate overnight.

+ The following day, remove the lamb from the refrigerator 2 hours before cooking.

+ Preheat the oven to 130°C (250°F/Gas 1).

+ Place the lamb in a roasting dish large enough to fit both shoulders. Drizzle with a little olive oil and pour in 60 ml (2 fl oz/¼ cup) water. Use two sheets of foil joined together to make a tent over the lamb, then cook for 2½–3 hours.

+ Reduce the oven temperature to 110°C (225°F/Gas ½) and cook for a further 4 hours. When ready, the meat will be very well done and falling from the bone.

+ Allow the lamb to rest for 20 minutes, then shred the meat from the bone. Place on a platter or divide among plates and serve with lemon wedges and a grind of pepper.

NOTES

Slow-cooking is brilliant with any protein. Invest in oven and meat thermometers — both are inexpensive, and will guarantee fail-safe roasting.

Serve the lamb with green salad, peas and potato or sweet potato purée.

Goat and onion curry

If you can't find or don't fancy goat, you can use lamb, beef or chicken in this curry — or go with lentils for a vegetarian option.

SERVES 6–8

+ Combine the goat, onion, sea salt, chilli powder, ginger, garlic, turmeric, vegetable oil and 1.5 litres (52 fl oz/6 cups) water in a heavy-based saucepan with a tight-fitting lid. Bring to a simmer over high heat. Reduce the heat to low, cover and simmer gently for 1 hour. Remove the lid, increase the heat to medium and boil gently for 10 minutes or until the sauce is very thick.

+ Meanwhile, place the coriander, mint, fresh chilli and lemon juice in a food processor and blend until as smooth as possible.

+ When the sauce has reduced, stir in the herb mix, and simmer gently for 3 minutes. Serve with steamed rice.

1.8 kg (4 lb) boneless goat shoulder (see Notes), cut into 2.5 cm (1 inch) cubes
8 onions, halved and thinly sliced
1 tablespoon sea salt
2 teaspoons red chilli powder
1 tablespoon finely grated ginger
2 teaspoons crushed garlic
2 teaspoons ground turmeric
125 ml (4 fl oz/½ cup) vegetable oil
1 cup coriander (cilantro) leaves
1 cup mint leaves
12 hot green chillies, roughly chopped
juice of 2 lemons
steamed rice, to serve

NOTES

Goat is available from specialist butchers. If you're using another meat, adjust the cooking time: longer for beef, less for chicken. Goat leg works equally as well.

These curries are great with rice pilaf (see page 185).

Roast pork shoulder with mustard fruits and aged balsamic vinaigrette

Cooking this delicious, moist pork shoulder on the bone will deliver the juiciest meat and the best crackling you've ever had.

SERVES 8

+ Preheat the oven to 200°C (400°F/Gas 6).

+ Rub the pork gently with olive oil, then give it a good rub with sea salt. Place on a rack in a roasting tin and roast for 30 minutes. Reduce the oven temperature to 160°C (315°F/Gas 2–3) and cook for a further 1½ hours or until meltingly tender. Turn off the oven, open the door and allow the pork to rest in the oven for 20 minutes.

+ Place the pork on a chopping board and slip a knife under the crackling. Remove the crackling in one or a few pieces and set aside. Slice the meat. You will need to slice around the shoulder blade, but it is easy and you can end up with rustic slices or chunks of meat.

+ Place some pork on each plate with some mustard fruits. Sprinkle with sea salt and white pepper and drizzle with aged balsamic vinegar.

+ Chop the crackling into pieces and scatter on top of the pork. Serve with a green salad and roast potatoes (see Notes).

1 free-range pork shoulder, about 3 kg (6 lb 12 oz) (ask your butcher to score the skin for you)
extra virgin olive oil
sea salt and freshly ground white pepper
200 g (7 oz) mustard fruits, sliced into wedges or left whole, if small (see page 194)
aged balsamic vinegar, for drizzling
green salad and roast potatoes, to serve

NOTES

The meat is rich, so I would usually serve this with a crisp salad and roast potatoes (you can parboil potatoes, rough up the edges and cook them with the pork for the last hour). Or, if you wish, you could serve it with potato purée.

Before you cook the pork shoulder, leave it in the refrigerator uncovered for a day. It helps the skin dry out and promotes a great crackling.

Mustard fruits

MAKES 750 G (1 LB 10 OZ)

+ Place the dried figs in a heatproof bowl, cover with boiling water and stand for 30 minutes. Drain and set aside.

+ Meanwhile, place all the ingredients except the dried fruit in a heavy-based saucepan and bring to the boil over medium heat. Bring to the boil, then reduce the heat to low and simmer gently for 15–20 minutes or until the syrup has reduced to about 375 ml (13 fl oz/1½ cups).

+ Add the figs, apricots and apples to the liquid, return to the oil, then simmer over low heat for another 10 minutes. Remove from the heat and pour into a hot, 1 litre (35 fl oz/4 cup) capacity sterilised jar and seal. Stand until cool, then store in a cool, dark place for up to 3 months. Once opened, the mustard fruits will keep, refrigerated, for at least 1 month.

100 g (3½ oz) dried figs
1 teaspoon yellow mustard seeds
1 teaspoon brown mustard seeds
1 teaspoon coriander seeds
350 g (12 oz) caster (superfine) sugar
100 ml (3½ fl oz) white wine vinegar
1 teaspoon hot English mustard
1 teaspoon wholegrain dijon mustard
100 g (3½ oz) dried apricots
100 g (3½ oz) dried apples

Penne with meatballs and fresh tomato sauce

Who doesn't love meatballs? These are just as good with beef or chicken mince, but the pork makes them extra juicy.

SERVES 4

+ For the tomato sauce, heat the olive oil in a large, heavy-based saucepan over low heat. Add the garlic, anchovies, chilli and a pinch of sea salt, and cook for 5 minutes or until soft. Add the tomato and cook, uncovered, for 20 minutes or until it is a nice sauce consistency. Season to taste.

+ Meanwhile, for the meatballs, soak the breadcrumbs in the milk for 5 minutes or until soft, then mash with a fork. Heat 1 tablespoon of the olive oil in a small saucepan over low heat. Cook the onion and garlic for 5 minutes or until soft, then remove and set aside to cool.

+ Place the pork, bread mixture, onion and garlic mixture, parsley, thyme, tomato paste and parmesan in a bowl and season to taste. Using clean hands, mix well so the mixture holds together. Form into small balls.

+ Heat the remaining olive oil in a large, heavy-based frying pan over medium–high heat and cook the meatballs in batches until golden and nearly cooked through — don't overcrowd the pan. Add all the meatballs to the hot tomato sauce and cook over low heat until heated through.

+ Cook the penne in well-salted boiling water, until *al dente*, then drain. Add the penne to the tomato sauce and meatballs and toss gently to coat. Divide among four pasta bowls and sprinkle with parmesan and a generous grind of black pepper.

350 g (12 oz) minced (ground) pork, not too lean
25 g (1 oz) fresh breadcrumbs
2 tablespoons milk
2 tablespoons extra virgin olive oil
½ small onion, finely chopped
1 garlic clove, finely chopped
1 tablespoon flat-leaf (Italian) parsley, finely chopped
pinch of chopped thyme
1 teaspoon tomato paste (concentrated purée)
1 tablespoon freshly grated parmesan, plus extra, to serve
sea salt and freshly ground black pepper
400 g (14 oz) penne

Tomato sauce

60 ml (2 fl oz/¼ cup) extra virgin olive oil
4 garlic cloves, thinly sliced
4 anchovy fillets
½ teaspoon mild chilli flakes
sea salt and freshly ground black pepper
1 kg (2 lb 4 oz) vine-ripened tomatoes, peeled, seeded and roughly chopped

NOTES

I like the lightness fresh tomatoes give the pasta sauce. But if it makes it easier, you can use tinned tomatoes (2 x 400 g/14 oz tins). The sauce will taste richer.

The springiness of the meatballs will improve if you work the mince a bit: slap the meat against the side of the bowl as you are mixing it. The proteins released in the meat will make it more gelatinous.

Fig and walnut cream cake

A decadent cake perfect for afternoon tea.

SERVES 8

+ Preheat the oven to 180°C (350°F/Gas 4). Line the base of a 20 cm (8 inch) round cake tin with lightly buttered baking paper.

+ Place the eggs, caster sugar and olive oil in the bowl of an electric mixer, and beat until pale and fluffy. Sift in the flour, baking powder, cinnamon and salt. Fold through the yoghurt, then the vanilla, figs and walnuts.

+ Pour the mixture into the prepared tin and cook on the middle shelf of the oven for 50 minutes or until a skewer inserted into the centre comes out clean. Remove the cake from the oven and allow to cool for about 10 minutes. Run a knife inside the edge of the tin and carefully turn the cake onto a wire rack and stand until cooled completely.

+ To make the icing, using an electric mixer, beat the cream, icing sugar and vanilla until soft peaks form.

+ When the cake has cooled, spread the icing on top of the cake.

NOTE

If you want to lift the richness of the fig and walnut cake, replace the cream with whipped mascarpone. It's totally over the top and lush. Additionally, a nice spicy cinnamon syrup would work well here.

unsalted butter, for greasing
3 free-range eggs
140 g (5 oz) caster (superfine) sugar
200 ml (7 fl oz) extra virgin olive oil
250 g (9 oz/1⅔ cups) plain (all-purpose) flour
1 heaped teaspoon baking powder
1 teaspoon ground cinnamon
pinch of salt
100 g (3½ oz) Greek-style yoghurt
1–2 drops natural vanilla extract
250 g (9 oz) dried figs, soaked in hot or cold jasmine tea for 15 minutes, drained and roughly chopped
115 g (4 oz/1 cup) walnut kernels, roughly chopped

Icing

500 ml (17 fl oz/2 cups) thin (pouring/ whipping) cream
150 g (5½ oz) icing (confectioners') sugar, sifted
1–2 drops natural vanilla extract

Passionfruit tart

Passionfruit has long been one of my favourite flavours in desserts. The sweet, acidic flavour screams Australia to me and it is a great match with anything, from lime to mangoes and berries. It is also just perfect as the hero.

SERVES 8

+ Make the filling the day before you wish to bake the tart (resting the mixture in the refrigerator helps prevent splitting).

+ Using a hand-held whisk, beat the eggs and caster sugar until well combined. Stirring gently, pour in the cream. Add the passionfruit juice and stir until well blended. Cover and refrigerate overnight.

+ To make the pastry, place the flour, butter, salt and icing sugar in a food processor and process for 20 seconds. Add the milk and egg yolks and process for a further 30 seconds until the pastry just comes together.

+ Turn out on to a lightly floured work surface and knead lightly for a few moments. Flatten on the work surface and form a disc. Wrap in plastic wrap, place in the refrigerator for 1 hour.

+ Spray a 26 cm (10½ inch) loose-based round fluted tart tin with cooking oil. Lightly flour a work surface and roll out the pastry until 5–7 mm (¼ inch) thick. Roll the pastry over your rolling pin and gently ease it into the tin, pushing the pastry in gently so it follows the fluting. Trim the sides and reserve the excess pastry for another use. Place in the refrigerator to rest for 30 minutes.

+ Preheat the oven to 180°C (350°F/Gas 4). Line the tart case with foil and rice, and blind-bake for 20 minutes. Remove the foil and rice, brush the pastry shell with the egg wash and cook for 10 minutes. Remove the tart case from the oven. Reduce the temperature to 140°C (275°F/Gas 1).

+ Return the tart case to the oven and use a cup to carefully pour in the filling. Bake for 35–40 minutes or until the custard is still quite wobbly in the middle (see Notes).

+ Balance the tart tin on a cup and remove the outer ring. Place the tart on a wire rack and, with a palette knife, slide the tart off the base. Invert the pastry ring back onto the tart to help hold in the sides as it cools. Allow it to cool for 1 hour. Dust with icing sugar if you like and serve (use a serrated knife to cut the tart).

9 free-range eggs, 55 g (2 oz) each
350 g (12 oz) caster (superfine) sugar
300 ml (10½ fl oz) thickened (whipping) cream
350 ml (12 fl oz) strained passionfruit juice (about 20–22 passionfruit)
plain (all-purpose) flour, for rolling
1 free-range egg, extra, beaten with 1 tablespoon milk, for glazing
icing (confectioners') sugar, to serve (optional)

Sweet shortcrust pastry

250 g (9 oz/1⅔ cups) plain (all-purpose) flour
75 g (2¾ oz) unsalted butter, melted
pinch of sea salt
90 g (3¼ oz/¾ cup) icing (confectioners') sugar, sifted
55 ml (1¾ fl oz) milk
2 free-range egg yolks

NOTES

This pastry is ideal for making custard and fruit tarts. It can be made in advance and will keep in the refrigerator for a week. It also freezes well. The recipe yields one 26 cm (10½ inch) tart case or several smaller ones.

To make a wonderful citrus tart, replace the passionfruit juice with lemon or lime juice.

The tart should be halfway set when you take it out of the oven. If you take it out too soon, it will run when you cut it; if you leave it in too long, it will set too firmly and lose its elegance.

Bread and butter pudding

You can use plain bread for the bread and butter pudding, if you like. Just add a handful of raisins or sultanas that have been soaked in hot water.

SERVES 6

+ Preheat the oven to 170°C (325°F/Gas 3).

+ Lightly grease a 20 cm (8 inch) square ovenproof dish with butter (or you could use 6 individual ceramic pudding moulds, about 250 ml (9 fl oz/1 cup) capacity each).

+ Cut the crusts off the bread and cut the slices in half to form triangles.

+ Place the butter, cinnamon, nutmeg and 1 teaspoon of the sugar in a bowl and combine well. Lightly spread both sides of the bread triangles with the butter mixture. Layer the bread in the prepared dish in an upright fashion at a slight angle so about a third of each slice sticks out of the dish.

+ Place the eggs, egg yolk, milk, cream, vanilla seeds and remaining sugar in a bowl and whisk well. Slowly pour the egg mixture into the dish, a third at a time, giving the bread time to soak up the liquid before adding more. Place the dish in a deep roasting tin and pour in enough hot water so it comes halfway up the sides. Bake for about 20 minutes or until just set and the top is lightly golden and puffed.

+ Remove the dish from the water bath and serve immediately, or let stand for 20–30 minutes until cool, then cover and refrigerate for 8 hours until cold and firm, then serve. (This is equally delicious hot or cold.) Serve with crème Anglaise, whipped cream or ice cream.

400 g (14 oz) raisin bread
100 g (3½ oz) unsalted butter, softened, plus extra, for greasing
½ teaspoon ground cinnamon
½ teaspoon ground nutmeg
100 g (3½ oz) caster (superfine) sugar
5 free-range eggs
1 free-range egg yolk
200 ml (7 fl oz) milk
250 ml (9 fl oz/1 cup) thin (pouring/whipping) cream
1 vanilla bean, split lengthways and seeds scraped
crème Anglaise, whipped cream or ice cream, to serve

Raspberry panna cotta

Panna cotta is a classic summer dessert. Serve it with mixed berries or any seasonal fruit you like, and lots of it. The more, the merrier.

SERVES 10

+ Place the cream and sugar in a saucepan over medium heat. Bring to the boil, then reduce the heat to low and simmer gently for 5 minutes, then remove from the heat.

+ Add the strained raspberry purée to the cream mixture and combine well.

+ Soak the gelatine in cold water until soft, squeeze out the water, then add to the hot cream mixture. Stir well, then strain the mixture through a fine sieve.

+ Pour the cream mixture into 10 plastic 125 ml (4 fl oz/½ cup) capacity dariole moulds or ramekins. Place in the refrigerator to set for 4 hours or overnight.

+ To serve, dip each mould into a bowl of hot water for a few seconds. Run a knife around the inside edge and turn the panna cottas out onto plates or into shallow bowls. Place the fresh raspberries around the panna cottas and dust with icing sugar if you like.

1 litre (35 fl oz/4 cups) thin (pouring/whipping) cream
160 g (5¾ oz) caster (superfine) sugar
150 g (5½ oz/1 cup) frozen raspberries, thawed, puréed and strained through a sieve
3 titanium-strength gelatine leaves
fresh raspberries and icing (confectioners') sugar, to serve (optional)

Peach, ginger and vanilla pudding

SERVES 6

3 firm peaches
100 g (3½ oz/½ cup) brown sugar
200 g (7 oz) unsalted butter, softened
115 g (4 oz) caster (superfine) sugar
1 vanilla bean, split and seeds scraped
4 free-range eggs

1 teaspoon baking powder
25 g (1 oz/¼ cup) ground almonds
60 g (2¼ oz) self-raising flour, sifted
125 g (4½ oz) crystallised ginger,
  roughly sliced
lightly whipped crème fraîche, to serve

+ Butter and lightly flour a 1.5–2 litre (52–70 fl oz/6–8 cup) capacity
  ovenproof dish.

+ Using a sharp knife, peel the peaches, cut in half, then cut each half
  into 3–4 wedges.

+ Place the brown sugar and 60 ml (2 fl oz/¼ cup) water in a saucepan and stir
  over medium heat until the sugar dissolves. Bring to the boil, then remove from
  the heat. Add the peaches, turn to coat, then remove the peaches from the
  syrup and reserve both.

+ Preheat the oven to 190°C (375°F/ Gas 5).

+ Using an electric mixer, beat the butter, caster sugar and vanilla bean seeds
  until light and fluffy. Gradually add the eggs, one at a time, beating well after
  each addition. The mixture may appear to split but keep beating; it will come
  back together. Combine the baking powder, ground almonds and flour and
  add to the batter. Add the ginger and mix well.

+ Place the peaches in the base of the prepared dish and pour in the batter.
  Bake for 30 minutes or until golden and springy.

+ Serve the pudding with some of the reserved syrup over the top and whipped
  crème fraîche to the side.

NOTES

*The pudding can be made with many summer fruits — try nectarines,
apricots or cherries. I serve it with whipped crème fraîche, but it is
also cracking with vanilla ice cream.*

*If you want to do individual puddings, you can use 250 ml (9 fl oz/
1 cup) capacity ramekins. Make sure you line the bases with a round
of baking paper.*

Raspberry and pear cake

SERVES 10

+ Preheat the oven to 180°C (350°F/Gas 4). Line the base of a 20 cm (8 inch) springform cake tin with baking paper.

+ Peel, core and roughly chop the pears. Place in a bowl, squeeze over the lemon juice and toss to coat. The lemon juice will stop the pears from browning.

+ Using an electric mixer, beat the butter and sugar until light and fluffy and the sugar has dissolved. Add the egg, a little at a time, beating well after each addition.

+ Combine the flour and ground almonds, then fold into the butter mixture, in three batches. Stir in the milk, then gently stir in the raspberries and pear. Scrape the mixture into the prepared tin and bake for 1¼ hours or until a skewer inserted into the centre comes out clean. Remove from the oven, allow to cool in the tin, then run a knife around the inside of the tin and remove the springform. Serve the cake in slices with a dollop of whipped cream.

NOTE

In summer, try plums, apricots, peaches, nectarines and any berry. I like it with ice cream, and it also works well with whipped mascarpone.

2 ripe pears
juice of 1 lemon
180 g (6¼ oz) unsalted butter, softened
180 g (6¼ oz) caster (superfine) sugar
2 free-range eggs, lightly beaten
200 g (7 oz/1⅓ cups) self-raising flour
100 g (3½ oz/1 cup) ground almonds
2 tablespoons milk
250 g (9 oz) fresh or frozen raspberries
200 ml (7 fl oz) thin (pouring/whipping) cream, whipped to soft peaks

Mango ice cream with fruit salad

It's hard to beat the first mangoes of spring as you reacquaint yourself with a beautiful fruit that has been out of your life for the past eight months. Here, a creamy, rich ice cream meets a tangy fruit salad. If you don't have an ice cream machine, you really should get one; they are so inexpensive for the joy they can bring. You'll need to start this recipe the day before.

SERVES 4–6

+ To make the ice cream, purée the mango flesh in a blender until smooth, then pass through a fine sieve, forcing as much purée through as possible. Discard what is left in the sieve. Add 90 g (3¼ oz) of the sugar to the purée and mix to combine.

+ Warm the cream in a small heavy-based saucepan over medium heat.

+ Whisk the egg yolks and remaining sugar in a bowl until pale, then, while whisking continuously, gradually add the warm cream. Return the mixture to a clean pan and cook over medium heat, stirring continuously, until the custard coats the back of the spoon. Remove from the heat, and strain into a bowl sitting over another bowl full of ice. Stand until cool, whisking occasionally. Once chilled, stir in the mango purée. Refrigerate in an airtight container overnight.

+ The next day, churn in an ice cream machine according to the manufacturer's instructions. Transfer to an airtight container; store in the freezer until firm enough to scoop. Makes about 1.3 litres (45½ fl oz).

+ To make the fruit salad, cut the fresh pineapple and mango roughly into 1 cm (½ inch) pieces and place in a small bowl. Add the mint and lime segments and juice and refrigerate until ready to serve.

+ To serve, divide the fruit salad among chilled serving glasses and place a large scoop or two of mango ice cream on top of the fruit salad.

500 g (1 lb 2 oz) mango flesh
   (about 3 mangoes)
190 g (6¾ oz) caster (superfine) sugar
375 ml (13 fl oz/1½ cups) thin
   (pouring/whipping) cream (35% fat)
3 free-range egg yolks

Fruit salad

1 small pineapple, peeled
2 mangoes, peeled
4 mint leaves, finely chopped
4 lime segments, each cut
   into 4 pieces
juice of 1 lime

Spring feast

Spring is not just daffodils and poppies and the heady scent of jasmine; it's asparagus, early mangoes and the unrivalled aroma of roasting lamb.

Spring is all about resurrection, resurgence — and life. Sure, we know that in Australia we can eat lamb all year round but, when it comes to creating a true, tastebud-melting feat of home cooking, can there really be any substitute for a healthy animal that has gambolled on green pastures and grazed to its heart's content on springy new clover?

The first season's asparagus, broad beans, new potatoes and the wonderful subtlety of spring lamb, what a perfect combination.

MENU SERVES 8

Prosecco and fig

+ Cut the stalks off the figs and roughly slice the fruit into pieces. Place the fig pieces into a mortar with the cognac and gently crush with a pestle until it forms a purée.

+ Spoon the fig purée into eight chilled champagne flutes, top with prosecco and serve immediately.

2 ripe figs
60 ml (2 fl oz/¼ cup) cognac
2 x 750 ml (26 fl oz) bottles
  chilled prosecco or sparkling wine

Buffalo mozzarella, smashed broad beans and ricotta salata on bruschetta

+ Pod the broad beans. Blanch them in salted boiling water for 1 minute, then refresh in iced water and drain. Peel the blanched beans — you should have about 2 cups of double-peeled beans.

+ Place 2 garlic cloves in a mortar, add a pinch of sea salt and, using a pestle, crush the garlic to a paste. Add the broad beans and smash them to a rough purée, leaving some beans whole. Add a good grind of white pepper, the olive oil, lemon juice and parsley and mix through. Check the seasoning.

+ Brush the bread slices with extra olive oil and place onto or under a hot barbecue or grill (broiler) and toast until golden on both sides. Cut the remaining garlic cloves in half and, while the bread is still hot, rub the garlic into the bread.

+ Place a piece of toast onto each plate. Divide the smashed broad beans among the 8 toasts, drizzle with extra olive oil and grind some pepper over. Tear the mozzarella and lay it on top of the beans. To finish, grate the ricotta salata over the top and serve.

4 kg (8 lb 8 oz) broad (fava) beans
  in the pod
4 garlic cloves, peeled
sea salt and freshly ground
  white pepper
125 ml (4 fl oz/½ cup) extra virgin
  olive oil, plus extra, for brushing
juice of 2 lemons
2 tablespoons thinly sliced flat-leaf
  (Italian) parsley leaves
8 slices of sourdough bread, about
  1 cm (½ inch) thick
4 fresh buffalo mozzarella
ricotta salata (dried, salted ricotta
  cheese, available from
  delicatessens), to serve

Asparagus with braised tomato and chilli

+ Blanch the asparagus in a large saucepan of salted boiling water for 4 minutes or until tender. Remove and refresh in iced water. Drain and allow to dry.

+ Heat a non-stick frying pan over high heat and add half the tomato slices without any oil. Allow the tomatoes to sear and burn slightly on one side, then remove from the pan and repeat with the remaining tomato slices. Return all the tomato slices to the pan with the olive oil and, using a non-stick spatula, scrape the base of the pan to remove any cooked pieces. Reduce the heat to medium–low, add a pinch of sea salt and gently simmer the tomatoes in the oil for 1 hour or until saucy. Add the garlic and cook for a further minute, then remove from the heat, add the vinegar and chilli powder and fold through.

+ Cut the asparagus in half, add to the sauce and toss until just warmed through. Place in a bowl and serve with the roast lamb.

4 bunches spring asparagus, woody ends broken off
12 vine-ripened roma (plum) tomatoes, cored and sliced length ways into 1 cm (½ inch) slices
125 ml (4 fl oz/½ cup) extra virgin olive oil, plus extra, for drizzling
sea salt
4 garlic cloves, crushed
80 ml (2½ fl oz/⅓ cup) Forum red wine vinegar (see Note)
1 teaspoon chipotle chilli powder

NOTE

Forum red wine vinegar is available at specialist food stores and good delis or supermarkets. You can use other varieties of course, but be sure to use a vinegar of excellent quality — it makes all the difference.

Garlic, leek and zucchini

+ Bring a saucepan of salted water to the boil, then add the garlic, leek and onion and simmer gently for 30 minutes or until tender. Drain the vegetables.

+ Steam the zucchini for 20 minutes or until tender. Place the steamed zucchini in a bowl, add the boiled vegetables and season to taste. Add the lemon juice, olive oil and parsley, then mash the vegetables with a fork to create a warm salsa. Keep warm.

+ Divide the salsa among eight plates and serve the with roast lamb.

2 whole bulbs garlic, peeled
4 baby leeks, white part only, washed and roughly chopped
2 red onions, peeled and roughly chopped
8 zucchini (courgettes), topped, tailed and roughly chopped
sea salt and freshly ground white pepper
juice of 2 lemons
250 ml (9 fl oz/1 cup) extra virgin olive oil
⅓ cup thinly sliced flat-leaf (Italian) parsley

Boiled new potatoes with mint

+ Wash the potatoes and place in a saucepan of cold salted water. Bring to the boil over high heat, then reduce the heat to low and simmer very gently for about 30 minutes or until the potatoes are tender.

+ Drain the potatoes and place in a large bowl. Season with sea salt and white pepper, and add the mint leaves, olive oil and butter. Toss until well combined and the butter has melted.

+ Place in a bowl and serve with the roast lamb.

1 kg (2 lb 4 oz) new potatoes, skin on
sea salt and freshly ground white pepper
1 small bunch mint, leaves torn
250 ml (9 fl oz/1 cup) extra virgin olive oil
120 g (4¼ oz) butter, finely chopped

Roast leg of spring lamb

+ Preheat the oven to 200°C (400°F/Gas 6).

+ For the lamb, using a paring knife, make 2 cm (¾ inch) incisions in the lamb every 3 cm (1¼ inch) or so along the legs. Place a sliver of garlic and a small sprig of rosemary into each incision. Drizzle the legs with extra virgin olive oil, sprinkle liberally with sea salt and place in a roasting tin. Roast for 35 minutes or until the lamb legs reach an internal temperature of 55°C (131°F) when checked with a meat thermometer. Remove the lamb from the oven, loosely cover with foil and allow to rest for 20 minutes.

+ Place a lamb leg on a chopping board. Using the shank bone as a guide, hold the shank firmly with one hand (using a tea towel will give you a better grip), take a sharp knife and slice off the two obvious muscles (these are the topside and round). Now cut parallel to the bone, as close as you can get — remove the remaining two large pieces of meat. You will now have four nice pieces. Slice each one across the grain into 1 cm (½ inch) thick slices. Repeat with the other lamb leg.

+ Scrape any juices from the chopping board back into the roasting tin, swirl them around to mix together with the roasting juices and spoon over the lamb.

2 spring lamb legs, about 2 kg (4 lb 8 oz) each, with the hip bones (aitchbones) removed
8 garlic cloves, slivered
1 small bunch rosemary
extra virgin olive oil, for drizzling
sea salt

Acknowledgements

I'd like to thank a few of the usual gang who bring my books to life.

Sarah Swan and Will Cowan-Lunn who cooked this beautiful food and promise the recipes work.

The girls and guys from Murdoch — Laura Wilson, Kirby Armstrong, Robert Polmear, Christine Osmond and Paul Chai for making sense of the words and making it a beautiful thing to pick up.

Sue Fairlie-Cuninghame and Earl Carter for making the photography so amazing, simple and sophisticated, also nice to catch up.

Sally Webb, intrepid publisher who promised it wouldn't be painful and stuck to the promise.

My three daughters Josephine, Macy and Indy who make me laugh and love and understand that blood will always be thicker than water.

My wife who holds the whole thing together beautifully.

Index

Published in 2012 by Murdoch Books Pty Limited
Recipes first published in *Good Weekend* magazine.

Murdoch Books Australia
Pier 8/9
23 Hickson Road
Millers Point NSW 2000
Phone: +61 (0) 2 8220 2000
Fax: +61 (0) 2 8220 2558
www.murdochbooks.com.au
info@murdochbooks.com.au

Murdoch Books UK Limited
Erico House, 6th Floor
93–99 Upper Richmond Road
Putney, London SW15 2TG
Phone: +44 (0) 20 8785 5995
Fax: +44 (0) 20 8785 5985
www.murdochbooks.co.uk
info@murdochbooks.co.uk

For Corporate Orders & Custom Publishing contact Noel Hammond,
National Business Development Manager Murdoch Books Australia

Publisher: Sally Webb
Project Manager: Laura Wilson
Editor: Paul Chai
Food Editor: Christine Osmond
Design concept: Kirby Armstrong
Design layout: Robert Polmear
Photographer: Earl Carter
Styling and direction: Sue Fairlie-Cuninghame
Production Controller: Mike Crowton

A cataloguing-in-publication entry is available from the catalogue
of the National Library of Australia at www.nla.gov.au.

A catalogue record for this book is available from the British Library.

Printed by 1010 Printing International Limited, China, Reprinted 2012.

IMPORTANT: Those who might be at risk from the effects of salmonella poisoning (the
elderly, pregnant women, young children and those suffering from immune deficiency
diseases) should consult their doctor with any concerns about eating raw eggs.

OVEN GUIDE: You may find cooking times vary depending on the oven you
are using. For fan-forced ovens, as a general rule, set the oven temperature
to 20°C (35°F) lower than indicated in the recipe.

We have used 20 ml (4 teaspoon) tablespoon measures. If you are using
a 15 ml (3 teaspoon) tablespoon add an extra teaspoon of the ingredient
for each tablespoon specified.